# VANISHING TWINS

A

VANISHING

LEAH

# TWINS
## MARRIAGE

# DIETERICH

Soft Skull  New York

First Soft Skull edition: 2018

This is a work of nonfiction. However, some names and identifying details of individuals have been changed to protect their privacy, correspondence has been shortened for clarity, and dialogue has been reconstructed from memory.

Library of Congress Cataloging-in-Publication Data
Names: Dieterich, Leah, author.
Title: Vanishing twins : a marriage / Leah Dieterich.
Description: First Soft Skull edition. | New York : Soft Skull Press, [2018]
Identifiers: LCCN 2018022961| ISBN 9781593762919 (pbk. ; alk. paper) |
ISBN 9781593763060 (ebook)
Subjects: LCSH: Dieterich, Leah. | Gender identity. | Open marriage—
United States. | Non-monogamous relationships—United States. |
Married people—Sexual behavior.
Classification: LCC HQ980.5.U5 D54 2018 | DDC 305.30973—dc23
LC record available at https://lccn.loc.gov/2018022961

Published by Soft Skull Press
1140 Broadway, Suite 704
New York, NY 10001
www.softskull.com

Soft Skull titles are distributed to the trade by
Publishers Group West
Phone: 866-400-5351

Printed in the United States of America
1  3  5  7  9  10  8  6  4  2

For JDH

OVERTURE

# OVERTURE

During my ballerina years, I danced mainly in the corps de ballet. This is the term for the group of dancers who are not soloists. The literal translation is the *body of the ballet*, and as such, all the dancers in the corps move together, like synchronized swimmers. They are one body. But not even a body. They are a backdrop for the principal dancers. Just scenery.

In high school I was given the option of studying French or Spanish. I chose French because it was the language of ballet. *Pas de deux, rond de jambe, plié, jeté.* I'd been saying these phrases for years, but until I started taking French, they'd just been the names of steps. I didn't know what the individual words meant.

We all took pseudonyms, at the behest of our teacher. These were our French-class selves, the people we became when we spoke that language.

My best friend was also a dancer and renamed herself Giselle, after the main character in the ballet of the same name. Giselle goes mad after being cheated on by her lover and dies of a weak heart. In the afterlife, she is taken in by a group of female ghosts called the Wilis, who force the man who betrayed her to dance himself to death.

Because my best friend chose a ballet character, I did too. In school, as in dance, she was so self-assured, so effortless. I studied her movements, like learning choreography, and hoped that when I repeated them they would appear to be my own.

My French alter ego became Odile, a character from *Swan Lake*. Odile is the Black Swan, the villainous doppelgänger of the White Swan, Odette, who is really a princess turned into a swan by Odile's sorcerer father. In the ballet, both roles are danced by the same ballerina. I always dreamed that someday I'd get to play them both.

In *101 Stories of the Great Ballets*, George Balanchine calls *Giselle* the archetype of a romantic ballet. "To be romantic about something is to see what you are and to wish for something entirely different," he writes. In *Giselle*, the Wilis wear billows of white tulle, so they seem "part of the world and yet also above it." The ghostly spirit, the sylph, was ballet's symbol for romantic love—"the girl who is so beautiful, so light, so pure that she is unattainable: touch her, and she vanishes."

One-eighth of all natural pregnancies begin as twins, the book said, but early in pregnancy, one twin becomes less viable and is compressed against the wall of the uterus or absorbed by the other twin.

*Of course*, I thought. *I lost my twin.*

This was after I'd read all the other books. The books about sexuality. The books about marriage. The books about love. None of them comforted me like this book did.

The story followed a pair of identical twins who were struggling to grow up without growing apart. My husband and I were struggling with that too.

I read it in one day, in every room of the house, on my stomach, on my back, on my bed, in the yard. I didn't worry about the ants scaling my thigh, or the black widows living under the outdoor furniture.

One-eighth. I tell people this statistic when I tell them I'm writing about my search for the twin I never had. The number makes me seem less crazy.

"Suspicion is a philosophy of hope," Adam Phillips says in *Monogamy*. "It makes us believe that there is something to know and something worth knowing. It makes us believe there is something rather than nothing." He's referring to the suspicion that one's partner is having an affair, but the same holds true for the existence of my twin.

I've always preferred being in the company of one other person to being in a group. I'd thought this meant I was antisocial, but maybe it's a desire to return to the relationship I had with another person in the womb. That pre-person—my little mirror ball of cells.

ACT ONE

# ACT ONE

Maybe my twin would have danced ballet too. I stopped when I was eighteen. Maybe my twin would have kept going.

Because of ballet, I spent a lot of time looking at my reflection. In class, we crowded each other to dance in front of the skinny mirror, the single panel in the wall of mirrors that inexplicably elongated the images of our bodies. The teacher tried to spread us out but it was no use. Our only other option was to lose enough weight to look skinny in any mirror, and we tried that too.

Twelve years later, I sit in the dark behind a two-way mirror with my ad agency colleagues, watching a focus group eat hamburgers and talk about how they taste. It feels deceitful to watch people when they think they are alone with their reflection.

We like to believe that a mirror shows our truest self, but it rarely does. If you're right up against it, with your nose touching the glass, you don't see anything at all.

That was the way I pressed myself to Eric. And Elena. And Ethan. I was too close and could not focus.

In all the articles, twins separated at birth always seem to share incredible similarities and quirks, no matter how differently they were raised. They hold their beer cans with just their thumb and index finger; they have moles on the left side of their rib cages. Neither of them likes ketchup.

I thought if I met someone with disgustingly fast-growing cuticles who liked the smell of burned toast more than anything in the world, it would prove I'd been missing my mate.

If my twin was identical, it would have been a girl, but if it was fraternal, it could have been a boy or a girl. All this is to say I didn't know what I was looking for.

Giselle got a boyfriend at the donut shop where she worked and quickly experienced all of her sexual firsts without me. This threw off the comforting symmetry that had always made our friendship seem predestined. Suddenly I felt as if I were a foot shorter than she was. At sixteen, her parents allowed her to finish high school via correspondence courses so she could spend more of her day at the dance studio. She was gone. Jumped off the seesaw while I was still on it, letting me drop with tailbone-breaking speed to the dirt below.

Ever since we met in third grade, no one at school had uttered our first names separately. They were always linked with an *and*. Now there was an empty space next to that *and*, a vacancy. Sometimes the weather in that space was mild, just the breeze of her being whisked away. Other times it rained for days.

I needed to sandbag it.

But instead of filling this void, I chose to build a structure around it. I got up at 6:30 a.m., was at school by 7:25, drank a Diet Coke, ate a Granny Smith apple for lunch, and finished my homework during study hall before driving myself to the city for ballet. This schedule was a scaffolding around my terror of being alone.

Was it her I wanted? Him? The acts themselves? It was difficult to pinpoint the object of my jealousy. It was easier to imitate, so I got myself a boyfriend—a popular boy I snagged by fooling around with his friend to prove I was sexually available. It was an odd way to show my interest in him, but he was a teenager, and it worked. Anyway, I was just spackling the hole Giselle had left.

My boyfriend was a soccer player who wasn't interested in ballet or any arts, but it didn't matter. At the time, our mutual interest of sexual exploration was enough. He became part of my schedule too. We'd fool around from two to four o'clock in one of our bedrooms while our parents were at work. After that, I'd drive thirty minutes to my ballet school, stopping midway at a Dunkin' Donuts near the regional airport to get an iced coffee, adding skim milk and three packets of Equal. This low-cal, high-caffeine cocktail typically sufficed to keep me awake during the drive. Ballet class ran from five thirty to seven, and after that we'd rehearse for whatever performance we were working on until about eight thirty. I suppose I ate dinner when I got home, but I don't recall. In my memory, that part of the day drops off like a cliff.

Prior to the boyfriend, before I started spending my after-school hours giving long and poorly executed blow jobs and getting urinary tract infections from sex, I would eat snacks. Having a boyfriend took the place of those snacks. I no longer needed them.

And I got thinner. *Da* was all my Russian ballet teacher said as she poked my side, indicating she was pleased with my weight loss. We were always praised when we became less and less of ourselves.

The desire to dwindle was strong. It felt religious, cleansing, a penance for some sin I couldn't pinpoint. At the same time, I felt like a contest winner. But I knew I couldn't have done it alone. As I held the ballet barre, legs working furiously below the serene upper body, my teacher's bony finger acknowledging my concavity, I attributed my success to having a sexual partner, a playmate who made it easier to not nourish myself.

In the 1950s, my ballet teacher had been the prima ballerina of the Kirov Ballet. She was the Lilac Fairy in *The Sleeping Beauty*, as well as Odette/Odile in *Swan Lake*, but her signature role was *The Dying Swan*. It is a self-contained piece, a four-minute solo accompanied by piano and cello, depicting the last fluttering movements of a dying swan. There is a flickery film of her dancing this piece on YouTube.

We often did *The Dying Swan* at the end of class. She tried to teach us how to die, but we were too young and too American. We were never doing it right. *Nyet!* she'd scream, and clap her hands for the pianist to stop. She'd shout corrections in French, our only shared language, and I'd translate for my classmates. And when language failed she was physical. She pulled on our arms and slapped our butts. When I think of her now, drawing her gnarled finger up the side of my ribs, she reminds me of the witch in "Hansel and Gretel," wanting to eat me, though she rarely ate anything.

Vanishing Twin Syndrome. That's what the *American Journal of Obstetrics and Gynecology* calls it when a fetus in a multiple pregnancy dies in utero and is partially or completely reabsorbed by the surviving fetus.

This phenomenon has likely existed forever, but it wasn't until the late 1970s, when ultrasounds became sophisticated enough to detect twins as early as five weeks, that doctors began having the unnerving experience of viewing twin embryos one month, only to find a singleton the next.

The term *vanishing twin* was coined in 1980, the year I was born.

In Lawrence Wright's book *Twins: And What They Tell Us About Who We Are* I read this: If the less viable twin is not consumed, it "exists in a kind of limbo, compressed by the other to a flattened, parchment-like state known as *fetus papyraceus*."

Papyrus, like paper.

"Somewhere in the vicinity of twelve to fifteen percent of us—and that's a *minimum* estimate—are walking around thinking we're singletons, when in fact we're only the big half." That's Wright quoting a geneticist, so of course I believe it. I believe in percentages, in pieces of pie. But I don't like his choice of words: *the big half.*

I don't want to be *the big half.* It sounds oafish and ugly.

And while it can't be denied that the big half is the winner, the one who makes it out, it also means that losing someone is a consequence of growth.

Deadline.com: "VH1 Orders Competition Series for Identical Twins." This headline appears in my browser. It is morning, and I'm in my office at the advertising agency. My friend Alex, who works in entertainment, has sent me this link because she knows I'm writing about my suspicion that I've lost a twin. Lately, everyone has been sending me these kinds of links, telling me about movies to watch and books to read, tagging me in the comments sections of news articles. It seems they're all interested in twins now that they have someone to share their discoveries with.

I am alone in what used to be my shared office. On the other side of the room, the blinds are drawn and the desk is empty. I no longer have a partner, so there is no one to see that I'm reading this press release instead of working.

"VH1 is putting the bond between identical twins to the test with *Twinning* (working title), a 10-episode, hour-long competition reality series set to premiere next summer. The project, created and produced by Lighthearted Entertainment (*Dating Naked*), will feature 12 sets of twins going through challenges that will test their twin connection. (Reports of the incredible strength of the bond between identical twins include cases of siblings dating the same people, finishing each other's sentences and feeling each other's physical pain.) Through the challenges, sets of twins will be eliminated until one pair is named the twinners and walk away with the grand prize of $222,222.22."

While I appreciate the cuteness of *twinners*, I'm annoyed by the grammar mistake. It should be "until one pair is named the twinner and walks away with the grand prize."

A pair, while two people, is singular. This is the grammar I feel in my heart.

The fact that it's called *vanishing twin* instead of *vanished twin* seems to indicate that the disappearance is perpetual, not completed, possibly not completable.

When one twin comes out and the other doesn't, it's over, in a certain sense. But grammatically, the vanishing twin is continually fading from existence. This makes it harder to mourn, because the disappearance never really ends.

Another friend tells me about a man she once worked with who had a pain in his ribs that wouldn't go away. It turned out he had a cyst that needed to be removed. When they did the surgery, they found that the cyst was a teratoma—composed of bits of hair, teeth, and fetal bones—the remnant of a vanished twin. "He had his twin removed," she said, and to underscore the reality of this unbelievable thing: "He took the day off work to have his twin removed."

I asked if she could put me in touch with him. I wanted to see if he'd ever wondered about having a twin or fantasized about it. Was the cyst a shock or did it somehow make sense? Did he ask to see what they'd removed? Did he have a scar?

"I don't think he likes talking about it," she said. "I probably shouldn't have told you."

I'd never pictured myself going to college, and certainly not in the Midwest. I'd always thought I'd move to New York when I grew up. I'd be a dancer. I'd wait tables. I'd ride the subway and stare at the ads in the train cars.

In Indiana, the ads were antiabortion billboards. There were Greek letters on houses, and sweatshirts and sweatpants embroidered with I-N-D-I-A-N-A. I never understood why people needed their clothes to remind them where they were.

I'd gotten offers to dance at Ballet Florida and Cincinnati Ballet, places I wanted to live even less than Indiana. I hadn't gotten any offers from companies in New York. Indiana University was my backup plan, one of the only schools in the country that had a ballet major. I figured I'd go there for a year and then reaudition for companies and move to New York. My time in Indiana would seem like a dream, and then a memory of a dream.

I met Alex the first afternoon after my parents moved me into the dorm. I had wandered out of my room toward the elevator, thinking I'd take a walk around campus to see where my classes were, or go to the ballet studio and work out. I knew I needed to be in top shape for the first day of class, and taking even a few days off made me feel stiffer, less coordinated.

As I approached the elevator, Alex was there, waiting to go down. I noticed her body. It was lean and athletic, and she had thick hair, like mine. I always liked girls with thick hair; I felt I had more in common with them than girls with thin hair—hair that could be put up into a bun with only one or two bobby pins, instead of the half a pack I needed to get mine to stay in place. Alex seemed like more of a jock than I was, though. She had her key on a red and white IU lanyard hanging out of her back pocket, the same way the basketball players in my high school had done. "Hi," I said, initiating conversation. My mother had told me *not to be aloof.*

"I'm Alex," she said. "Wanna go to this ice cream social?" She laughed as she pointed to a flyer taped to the wall.

"Sure," I said, happy to have someone to follow.

The beds in the dorms were called extra-long twins, a longer version of the twin bed. In America we call the smallest bed a *twin*, whereas in England they call it a *single*. Calling it a single makes a lot more sense, since it's a bed for one person. Calling it a twin assumes there should be two identical beds. And often there are. Married couples on sitcoms were shown sleeping in them until the early 1960s. Even Lucille Ball and Desi Arnaz—who were married in real life—slept like brother and sister in their twin beds on TV.

Twin beds seem to imply that you should never be sleeping alone. That said, the bedrooms of many children, in the time and place where I grew up, had only one twin bed per room. But not mine. My first bed was a double, and had an antique colonial-era frame my parents bought because it matched our house, which was built in the late 1700s. The bed had four posts with wooden cannonballs on top of them. It was a rope bed, which meant it originally had a grid of rope to support the mattress instead of a box spring. In lieu of the rope, my parents used a piece of plywood. This bed had probably belonged to a couple in New England hundreds of years ago. Their children would've slept in the same room, in a smaller bed called a trundle that, when not in use, was stowed under the main bed. I've always wondered how the parents had sex.

For me, the double bed was enormous, the floor miles away. In spite of this, or maybe because of it, I'd jump out of bed and make my way down the dark, creaky hallway to my parents' room, standing at the side of their bed while they slept, their chests rising and falling in unison. Because I did this every night, my mother was never startled when she awoke to find me standing there, and would ask sweetly, *What do you want, honey?* I never knew.

There was plenty of space in my double bed for another child, but when I had sleepovers, my parents would pull out an extra mattress they kept under the bed (an homage to its earlier trundle) so my friend would have her own bed. I wonder why they didn't just let us sleep together.

When Giselle and I returned home for Christmas break, I went to her house, since her parents were rarely there, and we sat in the cold on her deck and smoked clove cigarettes.

"I met a girl," she said. "Her name is Sun-Li, and she fingered me."

I'm not really sure that's how she said it. I doubt it rhymed. But that's how I remember it—that she'd gone off to school, met a girl, and had been fingered by her. I assume she fingered her back, but I can't remember. I assume we discussed other things, like if they had kissed or touched each other's breasts before the fingering, but I can't recall that either.

It's the finger that sticks out in my memory. A finger points, and in this case, it points to a fork in the road on my sexual map.

I knew I loved Alex when I found out she sang the instrumental parts of songs. I'd thought I was the only one who did this. We'd sing every note of the two-minute guitar solo in the middle of Guns N' Roses' "November Rain," going *wee doo doo wee doo doo weeee uuuuu* in a high-pitched falsetto.

She also loved Phil Collins as much as I did. We'd blast "In the Air Tonight," not caring if it seemed uncool as we air-drummed madly and belted out its chorus.

One Sunday night in late January, Alex's high school friend invited us to a party at his fraternity. We brought our friend Anna, who lived on the same floor in the dorms.

At the frat house, we drank cold red wine and danced to hip-hop in the high school friend's room. He sat on the couch while the three of us danced in a line, sandwiched together, me in the middle, oscillating between Alex and Anna. We locked eyes with each other, challenging. We moved up and down, exploring each other with our noses and chins, feeling the warmth come through the denim.

With our eyes and hands, we asked him to join, but he waved us off. We began kissing, aware he was watching, but he fell out of focus, like the background of a photograph.

We moved to the couch where he was sitting, each of us straddling some part of him, our hands on the wall behind the couch, trying to entice him.

"Do you want us to take off our shirts?"

"No," he said.

We were surprised and not surprised. Alex had speculated that he was gay, but with all the forced homoerotic behavior going on in fraternities, it was hard to know what anyone's sexuality really was. We continued to make out over him, but it was clear he was uncomfortable, so we left him alone and walked home.

We went back to our separate dorm rooms. We lay down in our twin beds and went to sleep.

The next morning I instant-messaged simultaneously with Anna and Alex.

Anna: *That was fun, but I don't really need it to happen again.*
Me: *Right.*

Alex: *That was awesome. When can we do it again?*
Me: *Soon?*

I took a political philosophy class and the professor assigned Plato's *Republic*. I'd heard the word *platonic* before, to describe a relationship that didn't involve sex, but I'd never connected it to Plato. I searched in *The Republic* for the origin of this idea but found nothing.

I felt distanced from the idea of a chaste love, since my one real college friendship had become sexual. I raised my hand in class to ask what a platonic relationship had to do with Plato, and my professor said it was discussed in another book called *The Symposium*, which wasn't covered in the class.

At the end of the semester, he assigned Margaret Atwood's *A Handmaid's Tale*. I had the flu that week and was bedridden in my dorm, so I read the entire thing cover to cover in one feverish go.

Atwood says: "Perspective is necessary. Otherwise there are only two dimensions. Otherwise you live with your face squashed up against a wall, everything a huge foreground, of details, close-ups, hairs, the weave of the bedsheet, the molecules of the face. Your own skin like a map, a diagram of futility, crisscrossed with tiny roads that lead nowhere."

I underlined this passage. I dog-eared the page. Tangled in my dirty dorm linens, I felt the need to masturbate. These words drew me in and anchored me. For a moment, they ceased my perpetual motion, my constant seeking. I became the paper in my hand. Shaking and then still.

I order *The Symposium* as I order so many books, at work, with one click. When it arrives, I am pleased to find that it is very thin. I don't have much time to read these days. I spend most hours after I come home from the office tweaking scripts for ads about compact sedans, World War II video games, or the new brioche bun on a double cheeseburger.

*The Symposium* is the transcript of a drinking party. It's funny and boisterous, a bunch of poets and philosophers telling stories and debating the nature of love. When it's Aristophanes's turn to speak, he describes a time when there were three sexes: male, female, and a combination of the two. Each was descended from a different celestial body, which makes them sound more like planets than people.

> The shape of each [human] was completely round, with back and sides in a circle; they had four hands each, as many legs as hands, and two faces, exactly alike, on a rounded neck. Between the two faces, which were on opposite sides, was one head with four ears. There were two sets of sexual organs, and everything else was the way you'd imagine it.

Zeus wanted to divide these original humans in half to make them less powerful, and he bade Apollo do it "as you might divide an egg with a hair." I can't help but see this as an embryo dividing in the womb.

After they were split in two, Zeus ordered Apollo to turn the face and neck so that "man might contemplate the section of himself: [and] thus learn a lesson of humility." This punishment is also its own consolation. It allows us to face a mirror and imagine that we are gazing upon our twin.

*The Rite of Spring* is a ballet originally created by the composer Igor Stravinsky in the early 1900s for Serge Diaghilev's Ballets Russes. The music was experimental for its time, using bitonality—playing in two keys at the same time. The effect is brutal and discordant. It sounds like animals dying. The choreography depicts a group of pagans doing primitive rituals to celebrate the coming of spring. When it was first performed on May 29, 1913, at the Théâtre des Champs-Elysées, a riot broke out. The details of this riot are oddly mysterious, but many in attendance claim that traditionalists began to boo as soon as the overture began. Arguments ensued, vegetables were thrown, and nearly forty people were ejected from the audience.

An article in the *Telegraph* on the hundredth anniversary of the premiere wondered whether it was the music or the dancing that got people so upset. Musicologists speculate that it could have been the "pulsating rhythms" but that it was "more likely that the audience was appalled and disbelieving at the level of dissonance, which seemed to many like sheer perversity." Listeners were used to a certain order to the way notes were strung together. With *The Rite of Spring*, there was none. "At a deeper level, the music negates the very thing that for most people gives it meaning: the expression of human feelings. As Stravinsky put it, 'there are simply no regions for soul-searching in *The Rite of Spring*.'"

For an audience in 1913, the choreography was likely as disturbing. "There's no sign that any of the creatures in *The Rite of Spring* has a soul . . . the dancers are like automata, whose only role is to enact the ritual laid down by immemorial custom. An iron necessity rules everything: there has to be a game of Rival Tribes, there has to be a

Dance of the Young Girls, and an elder has to bless the earth. And finally, a young girl has to be chosen and then abandoned to her fate, which is to dance herself to death."

We performed *The Rite of Spring* at the end of my freshman year.

Since its debut, *The Rite of Spring* has been adapted by many choreographers. The director of our ballet program, a white-haired Frenchman, improvised his version as we went along. All thirty of us were in the ballet—freshmen, sophomores, juniors, and seniors. The twenty-three women played the roles of the potential sacrificial victims, and the seven men played the predatory sacrificers. We began with the first movement, which was an ensemble piece. The director showed us the steps with his body, instead of telling us with words. The atonal music, the odd time signatures—learning this piece was like a math problem. We counted the beats, sometimes eight per measure, sometimes ten.

During the first week of rehearsals, we never got past the first movement. The following Monday, he called my name in the hallway outside the studios.

"Can you come in here?" the director said, motioning to the smaller of the two studios. I followed him, expecting a lecture about skipping Pilates that morning. Instead, I saw Nils, one of the few male dancers, waiting for me.

"I want to do a little zing wis you two," the director said as he put a CD in the portable player on the floor. *A pas de deux*, I thought. He fast-forwarded through the first movement of the piece until he found the part he wanted. A single trumpet sounded a warning signal, long and mournful, a high-pitched foghorn. The entire string section returned the call, reassuring and full, as though nodding its head and opening its arms in reply.

He placed me in front of Nils and put Nils's hands on my shoulders, arranging us like mannequins in a store window. When the trumpet sounded, he instructed me to keep my feet in place and lean forward. Nils extended his arms until they were straight, creating an angle between the two of us. When he let go, I was to step quickly away from him, chin high, gaze focused on some point in the middle distance, as if I were sleepwalking. We weren't dancing together anymore; it was just me. Nils was set dressing, statuary. The next steps were a series of piqué turns en pointe, traveling in a large circle around him. I finished the turns at the trumpet's most plaintive moment, then shuffled back to him, awash in the ebb of violins and cellos.

"Good," the director said. To show us what to do next, he played my role, holding one of Nils's hands high above both their heads, the other hand out like a T, and kicked his leg up to the side. It was comical, a man in his seventies, in a loose button-down shirt and a pair of chinos and sneakers, being partnered by this nineteen-year-old boy. After these kicks, the music changed, and he told Nils to let go so that I could be absorbed back into the crowd.

Later that afternoon, when it was time for the main rehearsal, the director had me do my solo in front of everyone. It was wonderful to spend the first movement of the ballet gyrating with the great mass of dancers and then to be thrust to the center, born into the spotlight.

"Very good," he said, and everyone remained silent.

"Zhanette," he said, and turned to extend his hand to Jeanette, a senior, as though asking her to dance. She took his hand and made a show of looking bashful—a half smile, eyes downcast.

"Zhanette eez going to be za sacrificee," he said.

I did not let my disappointment show. My face was serene, my posture good. I'd thought I was going to be the main sacrificial victim. The lead. Instead, my small solo was just a prelude to her being chosen. The sacrificer was trying me out to see if I'd be good to kill. It turned out I wasn't.

A ballerina is never supposed to show that she is in pain, though she frequently is. Some of the pain lessens over time, the stronger you get, the more flexible you become. Then, ballet can be transcendent. But no matter how good you are, there are still moments of great pain. There are falls, of course, but it's the invisible things that plague: tendonitis, bursitis, stress fractures.

Beneath the peach satin of the ballerina's pointe shoes are layers of canvas stiffened with glue that make the toe box strong enough to stand on. Between the canvas and glue and the flesh of her bunioned feet are the nylon mesh of her tights and the lamb's wool toe pad, felted by sweat. Quite often there is blood. Blisters form, swell, and then burst, sometimes in a matter of minutes—sometimes in class or rehearsal, and sometimes onstage.

We cut slits in the bottoms of the feet of our tights so we could access these wounds quickly, sitting down on the dusty floor in the wings offstage. We tried Band-Aids, gel pads, more lamb's wool, tape. None of it helped much. We plastered smiles across our faces and went back onstage, our eyes sparkling. The audience never knew. This was just as important a skill as an arabesque, a fouetté turn, a grand jeté.

Onstage, the large moon hung bright and heavy on the backdrop. The entire string section was buzzing, and we swarmed, running wildly away from our pursuers, hair flowing, arms flailing.

Horns stabbed the air. One! Two! Three! Four! On the fourth blast, fifteen women fell to the ground, each one at the foot of a man. The remaining eight women stood like the seven men did, arms in the air, palms up, as though trying to hold up the sky.

I was one of these women. We did not move. We looked down at our partners on the floor, our gaze calm and fixed. We were listening. A flute played as though speaking, pronouncing the time of death, as the spirits of the women ascended into the rafters. But the women on the floor were not dead. They rose to their feet, undulating like cobras, and we put our arms around them from behind, ensnaring them. In the silence at the end of the measure, they turned to face us, and we all took a collective breath. And then we began to dance.

The low boom of the timpani sounded the one of the four-count and the violins marked the other beats. *One* two three four . . . *One* two three four . . .

My partner was Sophia, my best ballet friend that year. We spent afternoons skipping class and ordering delivery from the local frozen yogurt shop. We smoked cigarettes out the window of her eleventh-floor dorm room. Despite the smoking, her skin was beautiful, never blemished. Her red hair made her white skin and blue eyes pale in comparison. She had no breasts to speak of, and not much of a butt. She looked like she could slide easily between two things.

Growing up, I watched reruns of the show where Patty Duke has an identical cousin, also played by Patty Duke. Under the credits, the two Patty Dukes play the mirror game. The theme song rhymes about their looking alike, walking alike, and talking alike.

Identical twin cousins are impossible, of course; twins can only come from the same mother, the same pregnancy. But perhaps this is too narrow a definition. What else do you call it when two people mirror each other? Maybe it's *twinning*, a perpetual state of becoming more alike.

The thump of the timpani kept time along with the low string instruments. With my back to the audience, I faced Sophia, locking eyes with her as we matched each other's movements, but unlike in the mirror game, we used the same limbs: my right arm, her right arm, my left foot, her left foot. To the audience, we were one body with four limbs. We never completely covered each other up.

The music changed. Horns shrieked and gongs shimmered like heat over asphalt. This was our cue to switch, for the women to assert themselves over the men. Now Sophia partnered me and I submitted to her, and it felt amazing to do this, to play the man and the woman within the same piece of music, in front of the same audience.

I think about how badly I wanted to dance a solo, to be seen and recognized. Wasn't that wish at odds with my desire for twinship? But there's a difference between having a solo and being alone. When you do a solo, there's an audience cradling you with their attention. When their backs are turned, you're alone.

My plan had been to quit college, but instead I quit ballet. It sounds almost accidental now. Some kind of administrative mix-up. As if I'd checked the wrong box and given up the thing I'd been doing for ten years instead of the thing I'd been doing for one.

It was the beginning of May, nine months after I'd come to Indiana, and I'd just danced *The Rite of Spring* in a beautiful theater built in the 1950s. A brutalist building with corrugated concrete interior walls and a rich red and pink carpet, swirled like a Pucci dress. The stage, large as the one at the Metropolitan Opera House, was the last one I ever performed on.

*I want to go out on top*, I kept saying. That's what I told my parents. That's what I told myself. I honestly can't remember what I told my teachers. I know that I called a meeting and I sat in their office and told them I wouldn't be returning.

*But you're getting so much better!* they said. *Who knows what you'll do next year!*

It didn't matter what they said. I wanted to leave on my own terms. Many dancers' careers are ended by injury, and I didn't want my physical body to dictate my career path. Nor did I want these crumbs of praise from my teachers to be the thing I kept coming back for.

I'd transcended the corps de ballet for a moment, and I didn't want to return to it. I felt exhilarated by my decision, the way ripping off a scab can feel good. The sting of your own doing. And that was how I left *the body*.

I had to choose a new major before I left for the summer. I considered nutritional science because I was intimately familiar with the calorie and fat content of most foods, but when I found out I'd have to take chemistry and physics, I reconsidered. My only other interest was writing, so, at Indiana, my options were English or journalism. One afternoon I pulled the clunky beige dorm-room phone onto my twin bed and called my mom for advice.

"What are you going to do with a degree in English?" she said. "Do journalism. It's a career." At that time, it was.

*I'm gonna put black paper over those mirrors*, my mother would say when she caught me looking at myself. She always told me I was beautiful, but she also told me I shouldn't be preoccupied with my appearance. *It's narcissistic*, she said when I asked what was wrong with wanting to look at myself.

We ascribe all vanity to Narcissus, looking at his reflection in the water, as though others throughout history haven't been interested in looking at themselves.

In Greek mythology, Narcissus is believed to have fallen in love with his own reflection, but the second-century Greek geographer Pausanias proposed a different explanation: Narcissus had had a twin sister who died. He had been in love with her, and gazed at his own reflection to remind himself of her.

Every winter my mother grows paperwhites on her sun porch. Small snow-white blossoms atop long, graceful stalks. Their Latin name is *Narcissus papyraceus*, like *fetus papyraceus*, the vanishing twin. They are both "parchment-like" but the *fetus papyraceus* is a complete narrative, a short but entire life compressed into a single page. The paperwhites are like tiny blank sheets of paper. One year she gave me some as a gift, but I couldn't make them grow.

"You have to meet Eric," a ballet friend from high school told me over the phone. "You would love each other." She was living in Colorado for the summer with her brother. Eric was their roommate.

"You're exactly the same," she said. "Artistic, smart, driven." I was flattered. "You're also both obsessed with your diets," she said. I wasn't sure if this was a compliment.

She built him up in such a way that I couldn't imagine he'd be real. She told me he'd taught himself to write code during his last semester of college, even though he wasn't a computer science major. She showed me his picture and said he'd done some modeling. He'd raced road bikes too, Tour de France–style. "He's also the nicest person you'll ever meet," she said. It was too much. I didn't believe one person could contain all these things.

A week after school ended, I flew to Denver, instead of home to Connecticut.

Would I know when I saw him? Would we finish each other's sentences? Have moles in the same places?

Inside the apartment, the afternoon light was fading. We heard a key in the lock, and when the door opened, there was Eric, with his tan forearms and champagne-colored hair. Even the blue of his eyes was somehow golden.

He had my posture—straight-backed, as though he were being pulled by the crown of his head, skyward.

My friend and her brother got off the couch to hug him, and I stood up too. He extended his hand to shake mine, and the hem of his T-shirt sleeve hung away from his body near the tricep. I wanted to stick my finger between the fabric and the skin to see if I could do so without touching either.

There was still snow on the ground in Rocky Mountain National Park even though it was May, but we hiked in our sneakers because that was all we'd brought. Halfway up the mountain, I thought it would be fun to throw a snowball at my friend's brother, whom I'd had a crush on in high school. I gathered a handful of snow, packed it into my palm, turned around, and threw it with all my might.

The snowball had barely left my fingertips when it hit Eric squarely in the face. He had been right behind me and had managed to turn his head at the last minute. His cheek was red and icy.

"That's quite an arm you've got on you," he said.

"I . . . don't have great aim," I said. "And I'm a lefty, so there was never a baseball glove that fit me in school, so . . ."

"I'm a lefty too," he said.

The others were a few paces behind us. We kept hiking and when we got to the top, we all stood shoulder to shoulder looking down into the valley. I wanted to look at Eric's face and was glad I had a reason to.

"Lemme see," I said. He turned his face so I could see the red mark, but he kept his eyes on me.

We drank around the fire. Eric and I shotgunned beers, a trick I'd learned during my year in the Midwest. We both knew all the words to "Nuthin' but a 'G' Thang" and we rapped them with awkward bravado. When it got later and colder, our friends brushed their teeth and retired to the tent, while Eric and I went to his car to listen to music. He played me things I hadn't heard: At the Drive-In, Digable Planets. We talked about our families, and while there were differences—his father was a teacher and mine a doctor; his mother went back to work (nights at a restaurant) when he was two and mine stayed home with us—there was one striking similarity: Both our parents had been married for twenty-five years. Most of our friends' parents were divorced.

I don't know how long we sat in the car. I was too infatuated to be tired. I wanted to touch his hand. I wanted to kiss him. But the armrest between us felt insurmountable. Eric said we should go to bed, so we quietly opened and shut his car doors. He found my hand in the darkness to lead me. His hand was warm and soft and firm and I felt a surge of relief. Hands, like kisses, could be bad, and ruin the chemistry. *This is the perfect hand*, I thought as we walked through the moonless night to the outhouse.

The trickle of my pee cut through the soundless air. I pulled my pants up, knowing Eric was waiting for me. The crotch of my underwear was cold. Wet with excitement.

We only had one tent for the four of us, and Eric and I lay beside our friends, who were either sleeping or pretending to. We began kissing and we did not stop, despite the siblings beside us.

We should have turned away and tried to sleep, but a magnetic energy held our bodies together as one body.

We spent the rest of the trip together. The siblings went about their business. My friend had to register for summer classes, and her brother was looking for a summer job. Eric was looking for a job too. Though he'd only graduated college a week ago, he couldn't afford not to work, now that he didn't have student loan money to cover his expenses. Luckily, it was the beginning of the first internet boom and anyone who could make a website could get a job.

One morning, Eric and I were alone in the apartment. After breakfast, he put on a collared shirt and I helped him tie his tie and wished him luck as he went off to an interview. It felt embarrassingly retro, as if I were a housewife sending my husband off to his job. But it was novel too, and I was grateful for a new role to play, now that I no longer had *ballerina*.

At the end of my trip, Eric took me to the airport and gave me *The Alchemist* by Paulo Coelho. He told me he'd underlined his favorite part. As soon as I was on the plane, I found the passage.

What the boy felt at that moment was that he was in the presence of the only woman in his life, and that, with no need for words, she recognized the same thing ... When two such people encounter each other, and their eyes meet, the past and the future become unimportant. There is only that moment, and the incredible certainty that everything under the sun has been written by one hand only. It is the hand that evokes love, and creates a twin soul for every person in the world. Without such love, one's dreams would have no meaning.

I turned the page back and forth. It smelled musty, like an attic.

I was always looking for other lefties, watching people's hands when they signed credit card slips at restaurants, threw balls, or cut with scissors. No one else in my family was left-handed, and neither were any of my friends, although this is not that surprising, since only ten percent of the population is left-handed.

"Both kinds of twins, fraternal and identical, have a higher rate of left-handedness," Lawrence Wright says, "and some scientists . . . have suggested that left-handed singletons may be survivors of a vanished-twin pair."

A card arrived in the mail from Eric. I opened it in my childhood bedroom and had to slow my eyes down to take in each part of the long rectangle. There was his tiny, almost illegible handwriting, and a collection of drawings he'd done in black ink and filled in with wide architectural markers. One drawing was of the Modular Man, a gestural outline of a man's body created by the architect Le Corbusier, for scale in designs, and another was the Golden Spiral—a spiral drawn inside a rectangle whose length and height are proportionate to each other at a 3:2 ratio, the golden ratio. The math was sexy, because I didn't fully grasp it, but also because it was rendered in muted golds and mauves, colors I was surprised a man had chosen.

I'd already sent him a card as well. Mine had a grid of squares I'd painted in watercolor. All but two were gray. We were the two matching red squares, I was trying to say. Everything else seemed drab by comparison.

The next month, Eric came to see me at my parents' house in Connecticut, where I was living for the summer. Any reservations my mother had had when I told her I'd fallen in love with someone on my one-week trip to Colorado disappeared when she met him. "He never stops smiling," she said.

Eric hadn't been to many museums. He'd been to national parks; he'd been to Indian reservations. During the week we spent together in Colorado, he told me about the tiny loom his dad bought him as a kid, and the beadwork he'd done on it. He pointed to a sculpture in the corner of the apartment that he'd made in architecture school—a red sawhorse with a suspension bridge made of piano wire hanging below it.

Eric had never considered majoring in art even though he loved drawing and painting. Like mine, his parents had directed him toward *something you can make money at.*

We'd lain on the futon in his living room after the first time we'd had sex, while the siblings graciously slept in the bedroom. I told him that in eighth grade, I'd considered becoming a performance artist instead of a dancer, after seeing a piece by Janine Antoni on a museum field trip. I recalled my twelve-year-old self watching a video of her performance, which involved using her head to paint the entire floor of the gallery with black hair dye. There was a video screen at the entrance to the gallery where she'd done the performance and a velvet rope across the doorway to prevent people from walking on the piece. I leaned into the room, my waist on the rope, trying to take it all in. The white walls, the large black strokes covering the wood floor. I would have liked to touch them, to trace my finger along their semicircular arcs, to get down on my knees and bend my head to the floor, to feel how it might have felt to do the performance, hair heavy and dripping, butt in the air, dragging the bucket of hair dye alongside me.

I took Eric to New York City because he'd never been, and suggested we go to the Guggenheim, knowing he'd studied the Frank Lloyd Wright building in architecture school. We didn't know anything about the exhibition that was going on, only that it featured the work of a video artist from the '70s and '80s called Nam June Paik. We walked up and up through the museum, curving ever so slightly to the left, spiraling skyward.

We'd seen paintings and photos in art history classes, and some sculpture too, but this kind of art was new to us. Large sculptures made of old TVs buzzed with an aurora of colors, lava lamp cubes with no stories.

"Thank you for bringing me here," Eric said. "I came to see the building. I hadn't even considered there would be something inside it."

Years later, he told me that this was the moment he decided to become an artist.

He sat on the edge of my bed, the one I'd slept in since I was five years old, and I went to him, putting my hands on his knees and parting them, to fit my body into the V they created.

"I love you," I said.

We'd only known each other a month. But this *I love you* was in my mouth, and if I was going to speak, it was the only thing that was going to come out.

"I love you too," he said.

The ligature *œ* has a special sound, the "open-mid-front-rounded vowel," which is something between an *uh* and an *er*. In French, you need it to make words like *sœur* and *cœur*. Sister and heart. It is taught to schoolchildren as *o et e collés*—*o* and *e* glued together.

I identify with this ligature. I see it and think *that's me*, though I realize this is strange. Why not my initials? The monogram that graced my grade-school L.L.Bean backpack?

In French class I had cast myself as Odile, the doppelgänger. The *O* looking for her *E*.

I had found him.

Eric and I spent my sophomore year visiting each other while I continued school in Indiana as a journalism student. I had no contact with my former ballerina friends. I spent all my time with Alex and the other girls in my dorm. I didn't go to any ballet performances, but I still liked to be on display. At parties, I'd find the highest place in the room and climb up to it, gyrating like a go-go girl, safely above the masses. I felt adrift and without purpose.

Eric came to visit me, and one drunken night, Alex and I reenacted our make-out scene with him. We were excited to have a willing male participant, as at that point it was impossible to fathom drawing a straight line between the two of us, to kiss each other without a third point to give shape to our desire. My attraction to Eric was stronger than anything I'd felt before, and the newness and novelty of touching Alex was endlessly intriguing. It was both strange and familiar. Lubricated by a healthy serving of Olde English malt liquor, we triangulated in ecstasy.

Now that ballet wasn't keeping me in Indiana, I felt little attachment to the place. The pull of my twinship with Eric was stronger, so I asked my parents if I could move in with him after my sophomore year was up. I needed permission because it wasn't just moving in with him; it was moving across the country and transferring to another school, and I needed their money to do so. On the sun porch of their house, where my mother kept the paperwhites, she told me, "Relationships are more important than anything else. Work comes and goes. People are what's important."

In our new shared space—a single bedroom, a double bed—Eric and I became incredibly attached. We had sex every day, as many times as possible. We went to sleep at the same time. Woke together, showered together. Our bodies could never be far from each other.

I'd kiss him goodbye in the doorway before he left for his job at the internet start-up just as I had that morning before his interview. I'd close the door after he left, only to open it again a minute later and run out to the car, hoping to catch him before he pulled out of his parking space. I'd open the door and sit on his lap, kissing him while he laughed. Was my desperation endearing? I'd slyly reach down and lay his seat back, putting us instantly horizontal, and we'd continue kissing and laughing.

By a stroke of luck or administrative oversight, my advanced ballet classes in Indiana had fulfilled all my upper-division humanities requirements in Colorado, so I took a lot of freshman-level classes. All the 101s: Astronomy, Philosophy, and my favorite, a sociology class called Social Construction of Sexuality.

I didn't make many friends at school. I was so focused on my relationship with Eric that I didn't have time to invest in others. I studied him. I tried to do the things he did. We bought me a mountain bike and special shoes to clip into the pedals. It was terrifying to be attached to the bike like that. I wasn't experienced enough to pull my foot out quickly, so I'd tip over, feet still attached to the pedals, helpless. Eric tried to give me pointers; he encouraged me. But my tears and frustration told him I would not continue. When we sold my bike, he stopped riding his too.

We did more of the things we both liked to do: vegan breakfasts at the punk-rock diner, foreign films at the independent cinema. We drove to Denver to see Almodóvar's *Talk to Her*, about a female bullfighter and a ballet dancer, both in comas at the same hospital, and the relationship that develops between the two men who visit them.

I don't remember the plot entirely but I remember a surreal scene, a dream perhaps, where a tiny man inserts himself into a giant woman's vagina.

I had always wanted tattoos. I drew on my skin constantly as a child—I even tried to give myself a tattoo when I was fourteen or fifteen. It was one of my ballet friends' ideas. We used sewing pins to scratch a design into our inner heels. Mine was going to be a star. It seemed easier than a heart, which I also wanted. The heart's curves were too challenging.

I sat on the toilet seat, my foot up on the opposite knee, and drew the shape with a ballpoint pen. I traced the lines with the pin over and over, scratching the first layer of skin until it opened up and bled, at which point I went over the lines with the pen again, mixing the blue ink with the red blood. It took a few days to heal up, but when it did, I had a little tattoo. It only lasted a week or so, until that layer of skin sloughed off. My mother never noticed, as it was hidden under a sock, or a ballet shoe, but I showed it to my friends with pride.

I got my first real tattoo the day after I turned eighteen, also without my parents' knowledge. It was a rune, an ancient Scandinavian symbol for prosperity, which looked a bit like an uppercase *F*. It was on my lower back, hidden below the waistband of my jeans. I didn't fully understand the word *prosperity* at the time; I thought it meant well-being in a general sense. I was embarrassed later when I realized it meant *wealth*. My mother would have been even more upset about the tattoo had she known this. She had always taught me that to openly desire money was tacky and shallow. This was an easy position to have when my father was a doctor and we were comfortable financially. During my first week of college, I got another tattoo below the rune: a Celtic triskelion representing the three forms of woman—maiden, mother, and crone.

Tattoos done with black ink turn blue in the skin as they heal. Like bruises, they are visual proof of pain you've endured. They prompt questions about their provenance. I envied people whose tattoos were less discreet; people who had the courage to wear their pain more openly.

Eric didn't have tattoos and didn't want them, so I stopped getting them when we started dating, confusing my own body with his.

I hadn't really liked the journalism classes I'd taken in Indiana. In particular I didn't like going out alone to interview people for stories for the school newspaper. In Colorado, the journalism school offered an advertising major, and I liked these classes immediately. You didn't have to talk to strangers. You could call to them with quippy headlines and flashy visuals. And in advertising, you always had a partner.

In the 1950s and 1960s, an agency called Doyle Dane Bernbach was the first to put copywriters and art directors in teams of two. In the past, copywriters had written headlines and taglines, and art directors designed visuals to accompany them. Bill Bernbach's fraternal twin pairs worked together from the beginning of the process, which allowed the visuals and the words to work in tandem. In class we studied the first ad made this way. It was for the Volkswagen Beetle and is considered to be one of the greatest ads of all time. The tiny car floats in the upper lefthand corner of an otherwise blank page. At the bottom, a two-word headline: "Think small."

I spent the summer between my junior and senior year looking at Eames shell chairs on eBay. The shell chairs were some of the first pieces of furniture to be mass-produced. When they were introduced in the 1950s, they were cheap and egalitarian—a solution to the post-war housing boom—but now they had become collector's items and commanded a very high price. The originals were made of fiberglass and came in an array of sunny colors, most of which were now faded with age. I favored the DSS, the stacking shell. Besides stacking, the chairs could be connected at the side to create a chain, a long row, or a linked circle. Monday through Friday, I watched auctions for them, waiting for the right moment to bid. I knew about shock mounts, tags that indicated different production runs, Zenith versus Herman Miller, which colors were rare, how to spot a fake. I treated it like my job because my actual job was so boring.

I'd gotten a marketing internship at the tech company where Eric worked. Though I preferred my copywriting and art direction classes, corporate marketing internships paid, whereas creative internships at advertising agencies did not. I called my mother when I got the job, proud to tell her about the seventeen dollars an hour I'd be making. She congratulated me and said that because of the windfall, I'd be able to support myself for the summer.

I remember this conversation less as a dialogue and more as an image: me sitting on the floor of our bedroom in front of the flimsy full-length mirror, watching myself cry, phone in one hand, trying to convince her to at least pay my rent. I knew how spoiled I was acting, but the emotions still came, indifferent to my shame.

Eric had soothed me by promising that if I needed money, he could chip in extra for rent. I was pleased to find out as the summer went on that I didn't need it. He had been out of college for a couple of years and had made just enough money to buy a condo. Though it looked like a 1970s ski chalet with ugly carpet and wood paneling, we wanted to furnish it with modern furniture. The Eames chairs were the only mid-century items we could afford.

Toward the end of the summer, I finally won an auction for a large lot of twelve chairs. We rented a truck to pick them up. We had only wanted four chairs, but we couldn't afford to get four in mint condition. Most of the twelve chairs were damaged in some way; we thought if we could rehabilitate them and sell half, the chairs we kept would essentially be free. We ordered replacements for the ones missing feet from the manufacturer in Michigan. Some needed their broken feet extracted like teeth before they were fitted with new ones. Once repaired, we sent them off two by two to auction winners, mainly in Japan. I wanted to keep the pretty colors, but those were the most valuable, so I sacrificed them to the furniture gods, keeping two gray, an ochre, and a flawless red one for myself. Or, for us.

When referring to a couple one adds an *s*: the Smiths, the Kennedys, the Washingtons. Eames already seems plural.

Besides their furniture, I became fascinated with Charles and Ray as a couple, with the many facets of their partnership: lovers, oddly dressed design duo, filmmakers, utopian thinkers. One article makes note of the fact that they do not have individual Wikipedia pages, only a joint one. It also tells me that they died ten years apart to the day. Ray survived Charles by a decade. Her own power of ten.

"There's no I in Eames" is the title of a *Guardian* review of a book about Eames furniture. The book, by Marilyn Neuhart, aims to de-mythologize the Eames oeuvre as the work of twin geniuses. The rest of the office (including Neuhart and her husband) deserve the credit, she says. In this takedown, her descriptions of Ray are downright mean-spirited, claiming that Ray was not at all an equal partner in the design of Eames furniture and was "determinedly irrational, arbitrary, petulant and by turns, childlike and childish. She was also willfully eccentric, intensely undemocratic, and she made her own rules for herself and for everyone around her."

I'm depressed by a woman's desire to reveal Ray as some kind of fraud, as less than half of the Eameses. I'm also strangely encour-aged by her account that it was Charles who wanted the public face of the firm to seem like an equal partnership. Perhaps the balance happened in ways the studio employees could not see or understand.

In my gray cubicle at the tech company I studied images of their color-ful glass house filled with fuzzy textiles, quirky sculptures, and tum-bleweed hung from the ceiling, collected on their honeymoon road trip to Los Angeles. I had no idea then that one day Eric would get to tour this house, but that I would not.

The following summer, after graduation, I got a coveted but unpaid internship at an agency in Boulder and waited tables to make money. There were lots of writer interns, but only two art directors, and one of them was permanently paired with one of the writers. As a team, they won all kinds of awards, and I was convinced it was not just because of their talent, but because they had a solid partnership. The rest of the writers had to fight over the nonpartnered art director, or else cobble our ads together ourselves. The permanent team didn't have to expend any emotional energy looking for a partner. They could just get to work.

I daydreamed about ballet. I thought about *Swan Lake*. I'd never had the chance to play Odette/Odile, or perform with Eric in the audience.

One day I showed him a video of a performance from high school. It is a three-minute interlude for four dancers from the first act of *Swan Lake*, done entirely with their arms crossed in front of their bodies, each girl holding the hand of the dancer on either side, creating a sort of lattice. Our torsos weren't supposed to move at all, but our lower bodies were very busy. Our heads moved too, but they were always in profile, like presidents on coins, Egyptians on papyrus.

Eric asked me if it was hard to stay together. I told him the key wasn't the synchronicity of our legs but the way we held hands. If our grip was too tight, we'd bang knees, step on toes. Too loose and someone inevitably fell out of the lattice. When our hands were firm but giving, we were one body, a satin centipede moving back and forth across the stage. The *clop, clop, clop* of the pointe shoes almost military as we marched in an ecstatic tangle.

The first of the *101 Stories of the Great Ballets* is *After Eden*. It was first presented by the Harkness Ballet at the Broadway Theatre in New York, on November 9, 1967, and starred two dancers, Lone Isaksen and Lawrence Rhodes.

*After Eden* is a dramatic ballet about Adam and Eve after the expulsion from the Garden of Eden. It shows in dance terms, with no narration, something of the agony, regret, defiance, and resignation of the two lovers as they face the fate they had not imagined. In the process, their dependence on each other varies and it is this that makes the drama of the piece: Will they, after what they have come through, be able to stay together?

This is not a romantic ballet. There is no tulle, no white wedding dress looks. Both dancers are dressed in skintight one-piece unitards. They appear nude.

Lone Isaksen's obituary says she is survived by a son and her husband of forty years, Mr. Lawrence Rhodes.

*He won't fight with me.* That's what I told anyone who asked about my relationship with Eric. We'd lived together for almost four years. Anytime I got riled up—cried, raised my voice—he wouldn't dish it back to me. So I couldn't continue. It wasn't a dance. I was flailing, and he was still.

I decided his was the better way to be. Why did we need to fight? Couples who fought were doomed, I thought. Conflict meant there was something deeply wrong. My parents had been married for almost thirty years and I never saw them fight. I never saw them kiss, either.

*Even-keeled* is a phrase my mother might have used to describe Eric. She considered it a compliment. He was a ship that would not capsize. *In time, I will become this kind of ship*, I thought. *But, for now, I will anchor myself to him.*

There was a meteor shower. That's how Eric talked me up the mountain. The universe was throwing stuff at us like the snowball I'd thrown at him when we'd met.

He picked me up after my shift at the restaurant and we drove up Flagstaff Mountain to a scenic overlook. There was a small grid of city lights, and a vast darkness stretching toward Wyoming and beyond.

He brought me a salad and I gobbled it up hungrily. "Let's get out of the car," he said. "We don't want to miss it."

"It might be too cloudy to see," I said, with a mouthful of lettuce.

"Okay," he said as he reached under his seat. "I had wanted to get down on one knee, but . . ."

I looked at the small wooden box in the palm of his hand. It was a perfect cube, made of thin plywood veneer, stained a warm cherrywood color. I knew there was a ring inside, but I was fixated on the box. "Did you make this?" I said. He had.

I held it in my hand. It was all right angles, delicate and lightweight. I turned it over to see the paler unstained bottom of the box, nested inside the top.

"There's something inside, you know."

I laughed and opened the box. The ring was perfect too.

"It came in this horrible green velvet box. It was so cheap and cliché. I couldn't give it to you in that."

We'd been discussing getting engaged for the past six months. Eric was tired of his software job. He wanted to get back to making tangible things, so he had applied to an architecture master's program in Los Angeles and gotten in. While we were only twenty-three and twenty-six, and felt young to get married, we thought if we were ever going to do it, we might as well do it now: around his family, his college pals, and the friends I'd finally made in Boulder, my fellow interns and waitresses.

Even though I'd never been particularly interested in marriage or weddings, I'd drunkenly proposed to Eric a few times in the kitchen of our apartment, sloppily getting down on one knee the way I'd seen men do in movies. He always laughed these proposals off and said he'd propose to me when the time was right. We'd been to jewelry shops together, and I had always liked the small bands with tiny diamonds all the way around. No big center stone that screamed engagement. I knew I wanted to spend the rest of my life with him, but I knew I'd feel self-conscious about having a ring and a wedding when most of my friends weren't in serious relationships, let alone engaged.

The ring sparkled in the low light inside the car on top of the mountain. I slipped it on my finger. Once I had it on, I couldn't help but hold out my arm and admire it, the way I'd seen women do. I loved the ring, but I loved the box even more. The box was the symbol of Eric's love. He had cared enough to build something beautiful and unique to protect our sparkle. Something that was both sturdy and lightweight.

"Yes," I said. "To all of it. To everything."

Eric and I joined our first initials with an ampersand. It was the logo for our brand. We used it on everything for the wedding. The save-the-date cards, the invitations, the RSVP envelopes, the ceremony programs, the stickers that closed the cellophane goody bags of teeth-shattering candy almonds.

"I'm kind of seeing this girl," Alex told me on the phone a few weeks later. She had moved to Los Angeles after graduating from college. I was standing in the kitchen of our condo in Boulder.

"That's great," I said, frozen in place. "Have you guys, like . . ."

"Had sex? Yeah."

"Like, what did you do?"

"She fingered me, I fingered her, we went down on each other—all kinds of things."

We were accustomed to describing sexual acts in the frankest of terms, joking that we were like a couple of pervy boys when it came to sex and our sense of humor about it. I'd had a number of sexual encounters in college, before I met Eric, with various freshman boys who lived in our dorm, and older boys who had a thing for "the ballerinas." A group of my ballet friends rotated through three or four of them, or they rotated through us, each of us sleeping with one of them for a semester and then trading. I reported back to Alex in great detail about lumpy sacks and skinny dicks. I'd done cruel but comedic reenactments of their orgasm sounds. She laughed and cringed along with me, but didn't have any sexual experiences of her own to report during that year. And none the following year, in fact, except the ones I was involved in.

My stomach tightened as I listened to her so casually toss out details of sex with another woman. "That's great," I said again. "I'm so happy for you."

Eric wanted to go on a mountain biking trip with his dad. Their plan was to drive eight hours to Moab, Utah, ride the slick-rock trails, and either camp or stay in a motel. I didn't want him to leave me at home, but I didn't want him to invite me, either. I was terrible at mountain biking and not great at roadside motels.

In all the years we'd lived together, we'd been apart only a handful of days. Eric's parents lived an hour away, so he visited them frequently, and I always went along. We'd all watch the evening news, and his mother would do our laundry and fold the skimpy thong underwear I wore in those days into perfect squares, arranging them neatly on our bed. I always brought Eric with me to visit my parents in Connecticut. I was unable to conceive of family without him.

My resistance to his biking trip wasn't about being apart. I had traveled by myself to France while we'd lived together, but that had amounted to Eric handing me off at the airport in Denver to an old friend who picked me up at Charles de Gaulle. A relay race transfer, my body the baton. What I was afraid of was being left behind. One in a space meant for two.

Since I'd moved in with Eric, he'd never left me for one night. All 11,680 hours I'd spent in our bed had been beside him. Four years of sleep. I couldn't conceive of our apartment being just mine, even for one night. What would I do with all that space?

A few days before Eric's trip, I heard a sound. Tiny footsteps on the ceiling, running back and forth above our bed. I lay on my back, staring into the darkness. I felt as if I were in a ship's cabin, listening to a ball roll back and forth across the deck above.

It had to be something. Something in between the ceiling of our place and the floor of the apartment above. We lived next to a creek whose banks were lined with trees, so there was lots of wildlife around.

"It's gotta be a squirrel," Eric said.

"How did it get in there?"

"I don't know, but I'm sure it'll get out the same way."

It didn't. The next day we heard it again. It was above the kitchen in the morning while I made coffee and over the living room as I tried to read after dinner. Whenever I heard the scurrying, I had to stop what I was doing. All I could do was listen.

"Did you hear that?"

"Not really."

"That. Did you hear that?"

"I don't know. Maybe."

I heard it all the time. But I wasn't crazy. Sometimes he heard it too.

"We have to have someone come and look at it," I said.

"And do what?"

"Listen to it. Figure out what it is, what to do about it."

Eric sighed.

I found a name in the phone book. A man came the next day while we were both there. He was probably in his midfifties, short and sturdy. He wore a Dickies jacket with the name of the company embroidered on the left chest, and his name on the right: Mel. The three of us stood quietly in the living room until the sound of the feet moved across the ceiling.

"That's a rat," he said. "Only thing that could get in there. No way a squirrel could."

"So what can we do about it?" Eric said.

"I can fog up there. That'll kill anything."

"But won't it smell once it's dead?" I asked. That almost seemed worse.

"Not really."

I looked at Eric, waiting for affirmation, but got none.

"I'll give you a call," I said. "To schedule."

I couldn't believe Eric was willing to leave me alone with a rat in the ceiling. What if it got into the wall? What if it found a way into one of the cabinets and popped out while I was cooking?

"I don't want all those nasty chemicals in the house," he said. "Maybe it'll go away, and if it doesn't, you have the guy's card."

Eric's father came to pick him up the next morning. They strapped their bikes to the roof rack, and I went back inside as they drove off and stood in the middle of the living room, listening. I didn't hear the rat, but I was uneasy. I wasn't used to quiet.

I had to create some noise. I called my mother and told her about the rat and Eric leaving and my being afraid to be alone. Could I spend the night at a friend's house? she wondered. No, I said. Though I had a couple of friends, they were more like colleagues, no one I knew well enough to admit how terrorized I was by this invisible thing. I didn't have an Alex anymore. I had only an Eric.

My mother offered to put me up in a hotel. I sheepishly took her up on it. The offer was there, after all, and it seemed wasteful not to make use of it. I silently vowed to never tell any future friends about it. I assumed very few people would be interested in my less-than-confident self.

There was a hotel across the street from my apartment where my parents had stayed for my graduation, so I walked over and checked in. There is something comforting about being alone at a hotel, because there's always someone on duty at the front desk if anything goes wrong. Autonomy and security all in one.

I put my overnight bag on the bed and my wedding invitation supplies on the desk. I sat down and began embossing our logo on the paper. The embosser had a long metal handle to provide leverage, but the card stock was so thick I had to stand up and use my entire body weight and both hands each time I made an impression. It was boring, repetitive work, and I liked that. It allowed me to accomplish without having to think. I'd quit the restaurant because Eric had offered to support me while I focused on my internship. I'd seen that some of the other interns whose parents supported them were able to get a lot more work done. This time I happily accepted Eric's help. I loved spending the entire day concepting with my fellow interns, problem-solving, writing, and cracking jokes, but it was exhausting in a different way than the restaurant had been.

I flipped on the television to find something to accompany the work. ESPN was showing a cheerleading competition. I had looked down on cheerleading in high school (the forced peppiness, the cheering for sports), but I loved these televised competitions. *Ready? Okay!* one of the girls yelled. Techno music rattled the speakers as they moved into formation, nodding rhythmically at the audience with their shellacked ponytails and permanently raised eyebrows. Stripped of the pretext of a sporting event, the cheerleaders seemed to be encouraging me, letting me know it was okay to feel their energy in my body, the desire to be part of their pack, to move in sync with them.

I embossed in time with their cheers. Slide, position, press, remove. Slide, position, press, remove. An hour went by. My hands were sore and I turned them over and noticed that the handle of the embosser had made a deep red indentation in the center of each palm.

The competition was over, and golf was coming up next. I turned off the TV and felt embarrassed. I was a silly girl in a hotel across the street from her apartment, making wedding invitations and watching competitive cheerleading, all because she was afraid of an unseen rat. Even though my palms were sore, I embossed until I fell asleep.

The next morning, I went home. Sun streamed through the sliding glass door, creating a glowing rectangle on the carpet. I poured a bowl of cereal and sat in the rectangle, listening for the rat. I heard nothing. The sun warmed the carpet and it felt good. I stayed there for a long time.

Our wedding took place at the Boulder Museum of Contemporary Art, in a small gallery with white walls and black floors, much like the one I'd peered into at age thirteen, imagining myself as the artist, painting the floor with my hair.

Eric's aunt officiated and read the passage from *The Alchemist* Eric had given me when we met, six years earlier. Everyone said the wedding was beautiful. It was the first one I'd ever been to, so I didn't have a point of comparison.

I realize now that I didn't get married. *We* got married. Eric and I shied away from the "I do" of Western marriage tradition. We'd read about the Hindu marriage ceremony, which featured seven steps done shoulder to shoulder instead of face-to-face, and decided to do a version of that.

*Let us take the first step to provide for our household a nourishing and pure diet, avoiding those foods injurious to healthy living.*

*Let us take the second step to develop physical, mental, and spiritual powers.*

*Let us take the third step to increase our wealth by righteous means and proper use.*

*Let us take the fourth step to acquire knowledge, happiness, and harmony by mutual love and trust.*

*Let us take the fifth step so that we are blessed with strong, virtuous, and heroic children.*

*Let us take the sixth step for self-restraint and longevity.*

*Let us take the seventh step and be true companions and remain lifelong partners by this wedlock.*

We didn't have a sit-down dinner; we served only hors d'oeuvres, keeping people standing and hungry. We chose a jazz band instead of a DJ—no contemporary songs, and we expected everyone to dance.

The bandleader's wife was a champion ballroom dancer and teacher. Every Sunday for a month we drove to the untouched 1960s apartment complex where they lived and learned a choreographed first dance to one of our favorite jazz standards: "In a Sentimental Mood" from *A John Coltrane Retrospective: The ¡mpulse! Years.* Impulse with an upside-down exclamation point.

In the past, Eric had declined when asked to dance in public, but for our wedding he wanted to dance with me in front of everyone. "You're a ballerina. You deserve a proper first dance," he said. "But I need some help."

The teacher choreographed a basic routine that was meant to look unchoreographed. Once we knew the steps, I felt him relax. He twirled me and dipped me. The teacher put her hand on his back and encouraged him to soften even more. He moved his hips and loosened his grip. After we finished, she hugged us.

On the day of the wedding, she taught the rest of the guests too. She gave a swing-dancing lesson and all eighty of us followed along.

My favorite photo from the wedding: Eric and I holding one hand, our arms extended at shoulder height, pulling in opposite directions, gazing at each other from a distance. In the background, the adoring faces of everyone we know.

Another favorite: my dad, who also never dances, hands above his head in the air during our lesson, looking like a flamenco dancer.

Before we moved to California, we went on a honeymoon in France with money given to us by our wedding guests. On the train from London to Paris, I searched my French/English dictionary for words with *œ* in them. After *cœur* and *sœur*, I came across *mœurs*, the French word for *mores*. I couldn't remember the exact definition of mores, and with no access to an English dictionary, I had to speculate. I knew that mores were social things, codes, rules of some kind.

Monogamy is a *mœur*, I thought. An agreed-upon social code. An expectation of marriage. The word upset me. I loved Eric, sitting beside me on the train. He was my other half, my twin soul. But I didn't feel like having sex as much as I had in the beginning, and if I could only have sex with him for the rest of my life, did that mean I'd stop having it altogether?

The word *mœurs* was like monogamy itself—*œ* was the couple at the center of the word, surrounded by *m*, *u*, *r*, and *s*—*murs*—the French word for *walls*.

There was a jeweler next to the flat where we were staying in Paris, and that night it ended up in my dream. I dreamed that I purchased two necklaces, each one a gold letter hanging from a delicate chain. One was an *o*, and the other an *e*. I hid them in my suitcase and planned to wear mine the next morning. I'd wait for Eric to ask about it, and then, instead of explaining, I'd pull the other one out of my jeans pocket and hold it up for him to see. Then I'd stand behind him and put it around his neck the way the man does to the woman in ads. Even though Eric had never worn a necklace, I thought he might like this one. We were in Paris after all, and I thought it would remind him of the cyclists he'd grown up idolizing, the Tour de France riders who kissed their crucifixes after winning a stage.

I snuck the white box into the bathroom to put mine on, but when I opened it, I saw that the *o* and the *e* were no longer separate. They had fused, like the ligature, with the gold chains still attached to the top of each letter. I turned them over in my hand, dumbfounded. How could this have happened? It was summer, I reasoned, and there was no air-conditioning in our rented flat, but surely it couldn't have been hot enough in my suitcase to melt gold.

I knew I couldn't give it to him. I put them back in the box in my suitcase and hoped that when I got back to the States, they would magically detach from each other, that the spell would be broken.

We settled into a rental in West LA. A beige box on a street with one palm tree. I wondered how it would fare in a big earthquake, although it had no doubt been through many. I didn't have a job yet, but Eric had sold the condo in Boulder, so we had a bit of money to live on. He was immersed in school, so I spent most of my days at home alone, sending emails to creative directors and recruiters at ad agencies, looking at job postings and casting calls for music-video backup dancers on Craigslist, wondering if I was in good enough shape to audition.

When the Santa Ana winds came, the palm fronds sailed down, hitting the ground outside our bedroom window like percussion—a maraca or a tambourine being set down between songs. I didn't know the Santa Anas were *the* Santa Anas then. I just thought it was windy. It wasn't until a few years later, when someone introduced me to Joan Didion's work, that I understood they were a thing. She writes of the unsettling energy that accompanies the winds: "The baby frets. The maid sulks. I rekindle a waning argument with the telephone company, then cut my losses and lie down, given over to whatever is in the air."

Now that I understand the Santa Anas, and, along with Mercury in retrograde, the Saturn return, and other New Agey Californian phenomena, I am happy to have them to blame for bad things that happen and bad things I do. But even then, before I had ever called myself an Angeleno, I had begun to realize that even if it was seventy-two degrees and sunny most of the year, there was still weather.

Our apartment felt fragile. The walls of the two-story 1960s-era building were thin and lacked insulation. The windows were horizontal glass slats louvered to allow for ventilation. Jalousie windows, they were called. French for *jealousy*. We weren't sure what windows had to do with jealousy.

The jalousie windows were different from the thick glass windows of our winterized condo in Boulder. In LA, there was no way to seal ourselves off. The sea air had rusted the hinges on the louvers so they wouldn't completely open or close. We lay in bed at night freezing while our parents in Connecticut and Colorado scoffed at us when we told them we were cold.

*When are you coming homezo, schmookipoo?* I'd ask Eric as he went off to the architecture studio at school, where many of his classmates pulled multiple all-nighters. *Around midnight thirty, budzo*, he'd say.

Cryptophasia is a phenomenon where twins develop a language that only the two of them can understand. Many parents feel excluded by this, like tourists in a foreign land, unable to eavesdrop on the conversations around them.

We were fluent in the language of our own private country.

We didn't have a lot of furniture. This was mainly out of frugality, but also because of our lust for minimalism. We were inspired by the Barcelona Pavilion by Mies van der Rohe that we'd seen on a spring break trip to Spain, the apartment by Le Corbusier we'd visited on our honeymoon in Paris, and tours of the Los Angeles Case Study homes (including the Eames House) Eric got to go on with his class. The sofa we'd had in Boulder, a late-'70s hand-me-down from Eric's parents, did not come with us to LA. It was a boxy, rust-colored love seat with gold trim. *It's got good bones*, we said. *If only we could reupholster it, it wouldn't be so bad.* But it wasn't within our budget to reupholster. It wasn't within our budget to buy anything new, either, since we only liked very expensive, beautiful things.

Instead of living room furniture, we got a long, used library table to pair with our Eames chairs and put it in the middle of the apartment. It suited us fine. But not having a sofa did foreclose certain kinds of intimacy. There was no curling up next to each other. No snuggling during a movie or TV show, not that we had a TV anyway. We watched movies on our computers or went to the theater. The only place for intimacy was the bedroom, and it expected either sex or sleep.

*Let's do side by side*, I'd say if I wanted Eric to stop spooning me. In the summer it was because I was hot and needed space; other times it was because I was afraid spooning would turn into sex, which I didn't want but had a hard time denying. When we were side by side, on our backs, we pressed our ankle, knee, and hip bones together and held hands. It was like a lying-down version of the three-legged race in elementary school, but there were no opponents on the field.

At restaurants I'd slide in next to Eric if there was a bench seat. "We're lucky," I'd say. "Since we're both lefties, we can sit on the same side of the table without bumping arms."

"I wanna sit across from you. So I can see you."

"I want to be next to you, so I can look out."

"I'm having dinner with you. It's like you're not there if I don't see you."

"I'm right here," I said. "Can't you feel me?"

Architecture school was not what Eric had thought it would be. It was mind-numbing hours at the computer drawing straight lines; five-hour critiques; the possibility that after graduation you'd spend years designing bathrooms for some established architect, until maybe when you were in your fifties you'd have your own firm and finally build your own building.

His classmates didn't mind staying up for days at a time. They adopted the pretentious language of their teachers: *rhizomatic, interstitial,* constant references to DeLanda and Deleuze.

In his second semester, Eric took a class in the art department and discovered there was a master's program for media art. The students were making kinetic sculptures and interactive installations controlled by software. It was an evolution of the kind of work Nam June Paik had been making, which we'd seen at the Guggenheim when we first met. He wanted to transfer.

"What do you think?" he asked.

I thought about the night we'd spent on his futon in Boulder. His sawhorse sculpture, my performance art story. I thought about our marriage in the gallery, the wall text by the pieces listing the names of the people who made them, the media they used, the year they were created. "You've always wanted to be an artist, haven't you?" I said.

If he was my twin soul, did I need to ask him this? I could have just asked myself.

*It's like we're the same person. We finish each other's sentences.* This is what we've been taught to desire and expect of love. But there's a question underneath that's never addressed: once you find someone to finish your sentences, do you stop finishing them for yourself?

# ACT TWO

# ACT TWO

I sent my advertising portfolio to every agency in Los Angeles and had a couple of interviews. Eventually I got the call I'd been waiting for. I had been chosen. I was the one they wanted. But as it turns out I wasn't the one. I was one of the two.

The fatherly voice of my future boss told me my new partner's name: Ethan. *Another E*, I thought. He'd done a few years at a big agency in New York, won some awards, then taken a job in San Francisco, working for another prestigious firm. I pictured him with a beard, since it seemed that every man from the northern part of the West Coast had one.

The voice on the phone said Ethan raced road bikes in his free time. This detail made me reconsider. I knew cyclists. They were skinny and hairless. I thought of the Tour de France, which I'd watched with my father year after year. I'd ridden behind him on the old, unused twelve-speed he'd bought my mom. I thought of Eric, spandex unnaturally bright against the browns and greens of the mountains behind him. I guess I was destined to be with a bike rider, trailing him on some kind of imaginary tandem.

"Ethan's wife is eight months pregnant," the dad voice said, breaking my reverie. This news made him seem mature, masculine. I re-reconsidered the beard. "I'll take the job," I said.

After I hung up, I paced around the apartment and said my new partner's name under my breath. Ethan. Ethan. I tried our names together and wondered whose would come first when other people said them.

The morning of my first day, I put on a pale pink buttoned shirt, black jeans, and white Vans. I drove to the office and parked my car. As soon as I shut my car door, I heard that same fatherly voice. I turned and saw the man it belonged to, my new boss, David. He was tall and hearty. His skin was used to the sun.

We walked up to the front door and he swung it open, letting go of the handle, leaving room for me to glide in front of him. Inside, men and women hurried from one place to another, talking loudly and laughing.

"Wait here," he said, motioning to a bench in the foyer, and I sat down, feeling just outside the energy of this new family I'd soon be part of. No one looked at me; no one knew of my imminent joining. I heard David's voice again and stood up.

As soon as I crossed the threshold I saw Ethan, blue eyes shining, hand extended. It was rough and clammy; the grip was firm. I shook it, meeting his eyes as I'd been taught, and then looked down at our joined hands; our shirt cuffs. His was pink with white pinstripes. His jeans were blue. Their frayed ends grazed his checkered Vans.

Someone else in the room piped up, "You guys call each other this morning to coordinate outfits?" We all laughed.

"Nice to finally meet you," Ethan said, and I agreed, nodding my head too many times. His voice was high and lilting. *He's gay*, I thought. *But he has a wife.*

I was hungry already and wondered where we'd go for lunch. I wondered whether we liked the same food. The same music. Without having met them yet, I already felt different from everyone in the office. The girls all dressed up, the frat boys with backward caps, the volume of their voices signaling their confidence.

Even though I'd just met Ethan, I sensed there was something we shared, something that prompted my boss to put us together. I vowed to find out what it was.

I had to be at work before Eric had to be at school, so I always got up first. I made us smoothies for breakfast, and squatted down to look at the cups at eye level, making sure they were filled the same amount.

Occasionally I tried to feed him more. He'd often say he didn't need it, but sometimes after a meal, he'd go through the cabinets or the fridge, looking for something else.

He was taller than I was and weighed more, but he was so thin I could wrap my fingers around his ankle. *How are there bones in there?* I'd ask.

I was thin too, but something always told me I should be thinner. In ballet, the man needs to be able to lift the woman. Never the other way around. If the woman is too big, the man can't lift her. And if he can't lift her, she doesn't get to play the role—the Sugar Plum Fairy, the Snow Queen, the Black Swan, the Woman.

Lots of couples call each other *babe* or *baby*. Eric and I used those terms frequently, along with more unique pet names. But somewhere along the way I started referring to him as *the Baby*, and while the definite article made him my most important baby and, at least then, my only baby, the privilege of *the* was not sexy. It seemed innocent on the surface, though, and he played into it; his new role as the caretaken.

In the beginning, I'd been the baby. He taught me how to write a check and pay a bill. He supported me during my internship—things a parent might have done. Now it was his turn to be young.

We had begun to regress sexually too. We gave our genitals pet names and personalities and became ventriloquists. Eric's penis sounded like Beavis from *Beavis and Butt-Head*. He liked meat, red meat specifically, and was disappointed in Eric (whom he called Dad) for being a vegetarian. He liked big American trucks and longed to be adopted by a local Ford dealer, Big Mike Naughton, who appeared in TV commercials. I don't remember anything my pussy said. I can hear her voice, high and breathy, but I don't remember her having an opinion. I don't remember her wanting anything. She just deflected his advances like the cat being chased in the cartoon by Pepé Le Pew.

We had to stop this, I knew. We had to kill these characters. Even though we didn't talk in these voices when we had sex, it was impossible not to hear them. We needed to kill the Baby too.

Until this point, I'd never really critiqued our relationship. I didn't know the difference between critiquing and criticizing. I worried that pointing out a problem or removing a behavior would be like pulling the two of hearts out of a house of cards. I worried Eric would think I'd gone cold, but when I brought it up, he thanked me and agreed it was probably for the best.

Eric had desires undisturbed by the personification of our genitals. He wanted my feet. He wanted them bare. He wanted them sheathed. He wanted me to use them like hands and mouths.

Even though I had a far more intimate relationship with my feet than most people, I'd never considered them objects of desire. I was ashamed of them. As he was, for wanting them.

They were uglier than "normal" people's feet. By fifteen, I had bunions, which were always red and hot and refused to fit into strappy sandals. I developed a stress fracture in the talus, a foot bone I'd never heard of until diagnosed. I pronated, which meant my arches were falling, so the orthopedist made me custom orthotics, which thankfully fit into the clunky Doc Martens I wore in the '90s.

All dancers have ugly feet by conventional standards, so I didn't feel bad about their veiny-ness, their black toenails or blisters. But I didn't feel good about them either. They were not *good feet*, as far as dancers were concerned. They weren't flexible enough. They didn't have high arches. They were not feet anyone would have been jealous of.

Good feet were a thing. They were a distinguishing factor and a hallmark of success. *Oh, she has good feet*, we'd say. Sadly, they were not something you could will. You were born with them or not. You could work on your feet, and those of us who needed to did, but it didn't do much good. We sat on the dirty floor of the studio in our pale pink tights, before we put our pointe shoes on, and stretched each other's feet. One girl would extend her legs in front of her, pointing her toes toward the ground, while the other knelt facing her and pressed down on the toes with all her weight to see if they could kiss the floor. Mine never did. I wanted Melissa's feet. I wanted Carolyn's feet. They were stellar. When they were en pointe, their feet glowed like smoldering embers. Legs rising like smoke.

Eric liked tights and stockings, but I'd put mine away before we met. And outside the ballet world, tights required skirts, which didn't feel like me. But I tried. I wanted his desire to be my desire. I bought vintage panty hose with seams up the back and opaque toes and heels, sheer black versions of the pale pink ones I'd worn onstage. I couldn't get myself to wear them.

I didn't want this mismatch in our desire to drive a wedge between us, so I bought nylon ankle socks in brilliant colors: aqua with thin white stripes, kelly green with pin-dots, and a solid 1970s mustard yellow. I bunched them up into a ring and slipped them over my pointed toes. I wore them when we had sex. It was the least I could do. It was the most I could do. I was good at performing, and he was an appreciative audience and stage.

Though I tried to deny it, our differing desires troubled my notions of twinship, of coupledom. But more troubling was the fact that I desired something our specific pairing could not fulfill. I still thought about my Giselle and her Sun-Li, their fingers and hands. I thought about partnering Sophia onstage against the backdrop of the moon, and those nights in the dorm with Alex. They felt like beginnings that would never have endings, and the frustration of these unfinished narratives fueled my desire.

Some nights I closed my eyes and was back on the twin bed in my college dorm room, in a flu-induced fever of love for Atwood. *A Handmaid's Tale* teaching me the danger of complacency. "Nothing changes instantaneously: in a gradually heating bathtub, you'd be boiled to death before you knew it."

I began listening to self-help books about marriage. One book talked about desire needing distance. The author used the bridge as a metaphor. You have to cross a bridge to your partner, she said, implying that desire flowed beneath it. If there is no distance, there is no need for a bridge.

What this bridge looks like is probably unimportant. It could be heavily engineered, the kind people get master's degrees to learn how to build. It could be a tree limb, spanning a river, that you'd walk unsteadily on, arms out like a gymnast. It could be a rope swing you hang on to tightly, and if you don't make it to the other side, at least you're back on solid ground where you started.

Before we could build this bridge, we needed to grow the distance.

Sometimes conjoined twins are surgically separated. It's typically done very soon after birth; otherwise, they don't survive.

Eric and I had been together for six years. I'd have to separate us verbally.

"I want to sleep with a woman," I said. "But I don't want to lose you."

"I don't want to lose you, either," he said.

Maybe we could find someone to experiment with together, we decided. Sex seemed like a pleasurable way to begin a painful procedure. These words were just the beginning, a tacit agreement, a release form.

I assumed that merging my body with another person's body would help me to decouple from Eric. We didn't discuss anesthesia, the odds of recovery. We didn't know how much it would hurt.

We kept our eye out for girls we both found attractive, girls who were tall and thin with long, dark hair and dark eyes—my twin, essentially. This narrowed the field, but it was Eric's type, he said, and he wasn't really interested in looking beyond it. She also had to be single and interested in sleeping with a couple; a tall order.

There was an account girl at my office who seemed to fit the bill. She had just broken up with her boyfriend and wanted to let loose. She was tired of her businessperson persona and excited to befriend me, one of the creatives. She came to our apartment and drank whiskey with us and touched my thigh when she talked to me. One night we were at a bar together, and when she got up to go to the bathroom, I looked to Eric for approval before following her. I pushed her up against the dirty graffitied wall next to the towel dispenser and there was electricity in the wrongness of it. But the kiss itself was awkward—our teeth clacked together and the rhythm wasn't right. It was nothing like Eric and my kisses, but I held out hope that when the three of us were together, it might be better.

I never found out. A few weeks later, she began dating a man and declined my advances. She wanted to be a couple, not to sleep with one.

"Maybe I need to pursue this on my own, at first," I said to Eric. "Then slowly introduce whomever I meet to the idea of being with both of us."

"Coupledom is a sustained resistance to the intrusion of third parties. The couple needs to sustain the third parties in order to go on resisting them," says Adam Phillips in *Monogamy*.

It seems paradoxical, this sustaining and resisting. The conventional wisdom is to banish third parties so that we don't have to resist them.

"The faithful keep an eye on the enemy," Phillips says. "After all, what would they do together if no one else was there? How would they know what to do? Two's company. Three's a couple."

The first girl was Jimena. She was six years older than I was, but somehow she felt like a little sister—partly because I was so much more sexually experienced. She had never had a long-term boyfriend, or girlfriend. She was also seven inches shorter; hence, everything about her was smaller. Her feet, her hands, her fingernails, her mouth.

She did have two things larger than mine: her breasts and her long, black mane of Peruvian hair, which she kept hidden away in a tight bun at the nape of her neck. Walking beside her, I felt masculine in a way I never had before. I ditched my graceful ballerina walk and adjusted the way I carried my body to suit its new role as the larger person—the seducer and protector.

I met Jimena at a reading for a self-help book targeted at "straight girls" who wanted to have sex with women. This was a genius tactic for getting women with internalized homophobia to embrace their same-sex desire without having to label it as gay. Jimena and I both thought of ourselves this way, straight but interested in women, so that was the first thing we had in common.

I cringe a little when I think about it now. If you're a woman who wants to sleep with other women, you're not really straight, and cling-ing to that moniker only perpetuates the binary of straight and gay.

But calling myself a straight person who wanted to have sex with women allowed me to explore my sexuality without having to rupture my twinship with Eric. I could still be just like him—a straight person who wanted to sleep with women. It let me become more me without becoming less him.

After the Q&A, Jimena approached me and asked if I was going to have my book signed. I said no. "Are you going home now?" she asked. I told her yes, that I had to get home to my husband. "You're married?" she said. "Yes," I said. "But he's very supportive."

We exchanged email addresses and began corresponding daily. She was a graphic designer and liked books. We decided to meet for a drink. She emailed me directions to her house, and they read like this:

> Off Sunset Boulevard, across the street from the Mondrian, is Queens Road. You're going to take that ALL THE WAY UP. It's difficult to describe, all I can say is don't let the road lead you anywhere but STRAIGHT and UP. No veering to the right or left. You'll cross Hollywood Blvd. Keep heading up. Franklin will first appear on the left but you'll need to continue past and look for FRANKLIN HILLS estates (sign on the right—looks like a little subdivision). Head up that road (Franklin) till it zigzags and ends at the top. You'll see 1642 is a white garage. And living adjacent to that garage is me.

These instructions terrified me. When I moved in with Eric, I'd developed a fear of driving to unfamiliar places alone at night, though I'd never had an issue with it before. It wasn't until I met Jimena that I got over the fear.

I gripped the steering wheel as I drove up to see her the first time, turning down the radio, as though too much sound would send me over the cliff. I was afraid of going too quickly and losing control, and also of going too slowly and sliding backward down the hill, grinding the gears of my car and plummeting to my death.

At the top of the hill, I got a reward. From the patio behind Jimena's guesthouse, you could see twinkling lights laid out in a grid extending as far as the eye could see. Constellations on the ground. The lights weren't my only reward. I could try to say it more gracefully, but it wasn't that graceful.

It turned out that Jimena and I were both deathly afraid of STDs, so we followed all the precautionary measures. We used Saran Wrap for oral sex, condoms on sex toys, and short black latex gloves when we fingered each other. "I feel like I'm going to the opera," I'd say when I put them on.

Our barriers weren't just physical. I stayed merged with Eric. At home, in the bedroom of our apartment with no view, I crawled on top of him, feeling like a new person. *Yes*, I thought, *I still have it in me.*

I tried all the things I was doing with Jimena on Eric. They were things he and I had done at first, but had stopped doing years ago: kissing forever, undressing each other slowly, leaving our clothes on as long as possible. I asked him to put his fingers inside me the way Jimena did, except rawer, ungloved.

I introduced Eric to Jimena over drinks at a bar, hoping the three of us would hit it off. We talked about our families, and work, and books. We ate popcorn, drank Manhattans, and went home.

"She's sweet," Eric said. "But she's not really my type." This was fine because the next time I saw Jimena, she said that she liked Eric, but the idea of a threesome was too much for her.

"Is it okay if I keep seeing her?" I asked him in bed that night. He was on top of me, our bodies pressed together, our mouths inches from each other. I pulled at his lower lip with my teeth and ran the soles of my feet up and down his calves. He didn't say no.

It was easy to keep my sexuality a secret because I was married to a man. I thought Ethan might be dealing with the same dilemma, and I felt we'd be closer if we could share our queerness.

We had just finished a meeting at the office of the video-game client and were sitting in my car, not wanting to go back to the agency. When I asked him, without hesitation he said that he had been with men before. He'd been engaged to a woman at twenty, normal in the rural western town he'd grown up in, but his fiancée had cheated on him, so he'd moved to the East Coast to go to ad school. There he fell in with a group of gay guys who were nice to him. After school he moved to New York and went out every night with the guy he was dating. The G Days, he called them.

I told him about my arrangement with Eric and about Jimena. "I wish I could do that," he said, "but I don't think I could handle my wife being with someone else."

It was what everyone said. The assumption was always that both partners would do the same thing. I told him Eric hadn't been with anyone else yet, so I wasn't sure how I'd handle it, but was willing to try.

"Did it feel weird to be with a woman again?" I asked him.

"No," he said. "I definitely like women better sexually."

What was he doing with a man, then? I asked.

"I liked getting presents," he said. "I liked being taken care of. All the expectations are different, since it's two men. When you're with a woman, there's all this pressure to be the one to give them gifts and take care of them. It was nice to have that switch for a while."

I felt closer to him. I wondered which of us would take care of the other.

Whenever I told people I was supporting Eric, they raised an eyebrow. The eyebrow said, *Are you sure he's not using you?* I didn't think so. Eric had supported me after college while I worked on my advertising portfolio, and I didn't think of that as using him. That support had helped me get a job as soon as we moved to LA—the same job that would later allow me to help him focus on his art. In a way, investing in me was investing in himself.

*Support* may be too tender a word for what I was offering Eric. Perhaps all I was doing was covering expenses. And it wasn't as though the money came with no strings attached. For one thing, I'd asked for the open relationship.

I thought I could trade this freedom I'd given him to pursue an artistic career for my own freedom to pursue a sexual relationship with another person. I wanted an artistic career too, but as long as I worked full-time to support the development of Eric's, I didn't see how I could have my own. We couldn't both quit our jobs and be artists at the same time, I reasoned. So while I was the one working, I thought it was only fair that he do something of equal sacrifice for me. If we couldn't have sameness, then I wanted evenness. I wanted fairness. I wanted balance.

But what was on the scales, really? Money versus bodies? It is impossible to compare the two. They are different systems of measurement, like weight and mass.

*Are you sure he's not using you?* The answer was no. But was I sure I wasn't using him? As a mother, a father, an anchor, a life preserver, a safety net, a doormat? I did not know.

In a folder on my computer desktop I kept two photographs of Ethan and me sitting side by side in a giant twin stroller. In one picture, we're pretending to fight with each other. He pulls my hair and I smash his face with my hand. In the other, we're pretending to sleep.

The Manstroller was a prop for a commercial we wrote for a mini fast-food sandwich. Our spot involved two grown men in business suits being pushed in the stroller.

"Good job on that presentation today," the one guy says. The other guy smiles, accepting the compliment, but in a flash, his mood changes. He screws his face up and whines, "I'm hunnngggrrryyy." The crying is contagious, and the other man starts too. The nanny pushing the stroller talks to them in the voice people reserve for babies and pets.

"Awwww. You're hungry?" she says. "Here's your snack." She hands each of them the sandwich. A voice-over says, "Grown-ups need snacks too," and describes the product while we cut away to a close-up of it.

Ethan and I were proud of this commercial. We loved the giant stroller prop, and on set we thought the performances were hilarious. But once the commercial started running on TV, it wasn't so well received.

"Did you guys do that one with the guys in the stroller?" friends would ask, in a way that said *I hope not.* It turns out that listening to adults cry like babies is funnier in theory than in practice.

Even though people hated the spot, we didn't care. To Ethan and me, it was worth it for the photo of us acting like babies in the Manstroller.

We were tired of being the breadwinners of our families, the grown-ups, the caretakers, and jealous that our spouses could experiment—art for Eric, an organic baby food delivery service for Ethan's wife, with the safety net of our steady paychecks.

The Manstroller prop cost almost thirty thousand dollars to fabricate—more than the price of either of our cars. It felt good to waste someone else's money, since we had to be so careful with our own.

I spent most of my time with Ethan. Nine, sometimes ten hours a day, five days a week, in the same physical space. We talked about everything: the drugs he'd done before getting sober, our sex lives, our families, our finances, though we never told each other how much money we made. Ethan had made a rule of this. "Money does weird things to relationships," he said. I assumed he was referring to the dissolution of his last work partnership. I was fine being secretive or vague about how much we made; growing up on the East Coast had prepared me well for that.

At work, we used instant messages to talk to each other, so no one could hear our conversations over the cubicle walls. When we needed more privacy, we went to the only place within walking distance of the office: Swingers, a diner waitressed by tattooed girls in pleated mini-skirts and combat boots. A place stuck in a '90s version of the '50s.

Ethan became the best friend I never chose; my brother, my arranged marriage. We grew into each other, finding ways to fit the holes the other had. While he was tactful about money, he wasn't about much else. He offended people with badly chosen words and hasty emails. He was efficient, though, and incredibly detailed-oriented about his work. He made to-do lists and used his calendar. I was distractible and prone to procrastination, but I was also considerate and diplomatic. I could smooth things over with our colleagues when he'd wrinkled them.

One day I came across a catalog I'd purchased at the Louvre when I'd visited my friend in Paris before Eric and I were married. I'd bought the book to share with Eric, but now that we'd been to the Louvre together, it seemed like a pointless thing to own. Before I put it in a Salvation Army pile, I flipped through the pages and came across a painting by Théodore Chassériau called *The Two Sisters*. Painted in 1843, it depicts the artist's two sisters, Adèle and Aline, posed with their arms linked. Despite their identical hairstyles and gold and crimson dresses, the sisters were not twins. They were thirty-three and twenty-one when they posed for the portrait.

I was enchanted by this painting. The rich colors, the brunette women, the way their outfits and poses twinned them. I wanted to re-create this picture with Jimena, to commemorate our perverse sisterhood, but I needed Eric's camera and some instruction. I explained the idea to him and asked whether he could teach me to use the camera. He was busy with a project and said he would teach me at the end of the semester. "For now, it'll be easier if I just take the pictures for you," he said.

I was relieved that he could finally be included in our relationship, even in a nonsexual way. We drank whiskey on Jimena's patio overlooking the canyon and I was excited to share the view with him.

After the alcohol had loosened us up, Eric got out the camera and I posed Jimena and myself like the sisters, shoulder to shoulder, with linked arms. We didn't have identical dresses, but we imitated the body positions and expressions as best we could.

As he snapped the photos and later developed the film, I realized that I'd placed him in the role of my brother.

*Isn't he jealous? Isn't he upset?* everyone asked, with their words and their skeptical faces.

*I assume if he was, he would tell me,* I said. *I've given him every opportunity to do so.*

In truth, I didn't want to press him, lest he tell me something I didn't want to hear. I thought giving him space to react would be better, but I underestimated how much we both feared disagreement.

We liked discord in music—Stravinsky, and Ornette Coleman, the death metal he'd loved since high school—but we liked harmony everywhere else. Like nouns and verbs in romance languages, we insisted upon agreement.

"Where's the conflict?" my boss asked after Ethan and I presented him a script for a thirty-second commercial for a chicken sandwich. "Without conflict there is no story," he said. "Try again."

*Where's the conflict?* I mimicked to Ethan when we were alone. *If I had a fucking dime for every time I heard that.* I was frustrated, but I knew he was right.

*Where's the conflict?* friends asked about my relationship with Eric. They didn't believe there could be none.

I was upset that day because there had finally been some. I'd cut my hair from a feminine bob into a floppy Mohawk-mullet. It was something I could have never had as a ballerina.

Eric hated it. He didn't say so outright, but I could tell by the way he avoided complimenting it. And so I pressed on this issue. "It's a lesbian haircut," he said, and accused me of cutting it for Jimena.

"I cut it for myself!" I yelled. This didn't satisfy him, which I took to mean that doing something for myself wasn't the goal. I needed to do it for him or for us. I didn't realize then that my inability to bear his dislike meant I was complicit in this goal.

Jimena did like my new haircut, but she'd liked my old one too. There was no conflict with her, and I liked that. It felt peaceful to float in her ocean of acceptance rather than having to pass through the straits of Eric's.

There are two milestones in ballet training. One is graduating from soft leather ballet slippers to satin-ribboned pointe shoes. The other is dancing with a man. There was a class specifically devoted to learning this skill, and it was called Partnering. You didn't get to take this class until you were about fifteen or sixteen. You had to master all the moves on your own before you were allowed to do them with another person. Since there were fewer boys than girls, each boy had to partner multiple girls—raising the girl's entire body above his head, as if dead-lifting at the gym, or holding her extended fingers over her head as she spun on one leg like a top. Even though you were being supported or held in one way or another by the man, it didn't make the moves any easier than doing them on your own. In fact, it sometimes made it harder—your partner could knock you off balance. Your partner could make you fall. When you were dancing alone, you had only yourself to blame. This is why you had to be experienced before you could take Partnering. You had to master yourself before someone else could master you.

Eric spent a lot of time writing code, a cryptic language I didn't understand.

"Why do you love programming so much?" I asked.

"There's always a right and wrong answer," he said.

For his thesis show, he created an installation of colored threads, each attached to a motor in the ceiling in the gallery and weighted with a small metal washer at the bottom.

He programmed motion sensors to detect when people entered the space, making the motors spin, spiraling each of the threads into wispy tornadoes that bounced their washers up and down like yo-yos. The threads moved so fast they didn't read as lines anymore; they blurred and took shape.

At the opening, I watched from afar as people walked into the piece. I loved seeing their faces as the strings came alive. He had found a way to translate code, his secret language, into something embodied. Something that danced.

Eric was accepted to a prestigious art residency in the Maine woods. It sounded like summer camp, with cabins on a lake, communal dining, and individual studios for each of the fifty artists. The residency was three months long, and he'd been chosen from among thousands of applicants. I was proud of him, but looking ahead to my own summer—endless hours in the office, a two-week family vacation—it was difficult not to be jealous. Plus, I'd heard things.

The residency had an orgiastic reputation. "Would you be okay if I fooled around with other people during the summer?" Eric said. "You know, if it comes up."

*It's finally happening*, I thought. Jealousy tripped my insides, oddly indecipherable from the butterflies I'd gotten when we first met. "Of course," I said. "It's only fair." He asked how I felt and I said, "A little jealous. But that doesn't mean I don't want you to do it."

My relationship with Jimena had ended abruptly when a friend came to stay with her for a few months while he looked for his own place in LA. Even though she wouldn't admit it, I knew she hoped they'd evolve from roommates into a couple.

I wasn't sure if I was jealous of Eric being with other people, or being with other people when I didn't have anyone to be with, or jealous I wasn't going to an artist residency, a bacchanalian summer camp. Maybe it was all of these.

Eric said he wanted some ground rules, but I brushed his request aside, saying we should talk about things as they came up. In truth, I didn't want to give him ground rules because I worried if something was off-limits for him, it would be off-limits for me too. "Maybe no sex," I said. "Of the penis-in-vagina variety."

*Maybe* was my favorite word back then. It allowed me to live in *yes* and *no* at the same time.

Aside from one conversation in the car, Eric and I didn't talk about our arrangement during the remaining weeks before he left for Maine. We moved around the periphery of our apartment, avoiding something invisible in the middle of the room.

We were binary stars orbiting a common point called the center of mass, the center of our respective gravities. This center of mass holds the stars together but maintains their distance. They can neither get closer nor break apart.

During the first couple of weeks, Eric sent group emails to me and his parents: pictures of his cabin, the dock on the lake, images of the work he was making. He sent me separate emails about more private things. He told me about a night when he and a painter were talking about jeans, and she commented on how thin he was, that she could probably wear his, and he hers. Before that, they had been commiserating that, thus far, camp wasn't as debauched as its reputation, and they decided it was time to change that. They went into his room and traded clothes, their T-shirts and jeans, and then paraded around camp, inspiring the party-planning committee to throw a cross-dressing party later that week. After the novelty of wearing each other's stuff wore off, they went back to her room, took the items off one by one, and stood kissing in a pile of clothing.

I thought about this when I took off my own clothes. It required imagination, and made me realize how long it had been since I'd fantasized about Eric. I'd gotten so used to thinking of him as mine that I'd stopped thinking of him at all, at least as a sexual being.

I felt relief, as if his actions absolved my relationship with Jimena and evened things out between us. I was comforted by this evenness, but there was discomfort too, especially when Eric talked about her paintings, and how good they were. The competitive ballet dancer came back, the one who wanted the part, who wanted to be the best.

These feelings wrestled each other in a way that felt erotic. If I could keep this balance, I thought, everything would be fine.

Survivors of twin death often feel immense guilt. What they do with that guilt depends on the person, but often it pushes them to become larger than life to prove their worth. Elvis Presley had a stillborn twin.

*Don't be average*, a voice says. *Be exceptional.* I've repeated this mantra without actually saying it for as long as I can remember. Before words, I danced it. It is like a beat in my body, the tempo of my pulse.

The *average woman*, I thought, was jealous and passive: the sappy romantic, the cheated-on. I didn't question these received ideas; I just acted against them.

If I was average, how could Eric love me? How could he even pick me out of the corps de ballet, the tiny speck I'd been on the fuzzy VHS tapes of my adolescence? I nearly was invisible.

Instead of drifting back into the corps of women, I decided to cast myself as something else: the unfazed, the cool girl. Or not even the *girl*, as I had begun to disassociate with that term too. "There's only one girl in the creative department," someone at the agency had said of me, "and I mean, she's not really a *girl*." As sad as this statement seems now, I took it as the highest compliment.

What was I, if I wasn't a woman or a girl? A sylph, perhaps? Part of this world, yet also above it? But no, the sylph is too ethereal, too romantic. I would be the automaton of *The Rite of Spring*. I would be modern. A superior human who wasn't bogged down by emotions.

Ethan and I were shooting a commercial on a soundstage when I felt a strange itching on my spine a few inches above my waist. I reached my hand around and felt a small raised lump.

"Can you look at it?" I asked Ethan, lifting the back of my sweatshirt. "Is it red?"

"Yeah," he said, running his finger over it. "It's like a flat red bump. Maybe a spider bite?"

I didn't think so because I'd been wearing three layers of clothing all day as it was freezing on the darkened stage. I continued to finger the lump over the next couple of hours until it was time to go home.

By the time I got home, I also had a strange feeling in my ribs, kind of like a stitch in my side, as though I'd run a race or pulled a muscle, even though all I'd done that day was sit. I wanted to call Eric but it was impossible to reach him. There was no cell reception at the residency, and he could only access Wi-Fi in the library where he went once a day.

I called my father instead, glad to have a reason to speak to him directly. Nearly all of my phone calls home were to my mother, who relayed the salient details of our conversations to him. My relationship with my father had never been incredibly verbal. It was the care he took when examining my lumps and bumps that made me feel loved and connected to him. He once drained an infected wound on my head, a wound I'd gotten after a piano bench leg had given out while I was standing on it, trying to kill a spider. The scab had finally fallen off, but underneath it lay a tender squishy slug, which burst the moment he injected my scalp with novocaine. My mother had acted as scrub nurse, cleaned the puss off my bedroom wallpaper. I remember this scene as a kind of slapstick comedy. It was funny and tender, not gruesome. I had put myself into his hands and he had taken care of me while my mother stood at a certain remove, doing what was necessary. It was the opposite of my parent's usual roles.

"If you draw a line from the lump on your back to the pain in your ribs, are they at the same latitude, so to speak?" my father asked.

I traced my finger from the spider bite to the rib pain and sure enough, they matched.

"I think you might have shingles," he said.

Shingles sounded like something you'd get at a hardware store rather than something on your body. I imagined myself in a tube dress of asphalt ones, modeling them on the red carpet in some kind of avant-garde fashion statement.

He told me to get to a doctor as soon as possible because if I took Valtrex within the first seventy-two hours I could shorten the duration of the outbreak. I was mortified. *Valtrex* and *outbreak*: these were herpes words. I heard the voiceover from the advertisements for the drug in my head.

"Are they contagious?" I asked, wondering who I'd gotten them from and who I might have given them to.

"Not really," he said, and explained that shingles was the chicken pox virus, which I'd had when I was five, lying dormant in my body and deciding to reawaken in a particular nerve. My shingles could give chicken pox to someone who hadn't had them, but I couldn't give shingles to anyone. You could only get shingles from yourself.

I was concerned that it would be more than twenty-four hours before I could get a doctor's appointment so he prescribed me the Valtrex on his own and I took the first pill that evening.

I was glad I did because hours later the pain in my ribs was much worse, eclipsing the "spider bite," which was definitely not a spider bite, but just the first of the shingles lesions. Smaller ones cropped up underneath my right rib. After examining me the next day, my doctor said I was lucky to have already taken the first dose of medication.

"What does the pain feel like?" she asked me.

"Like someone is stabbing me with little knives from inside my body."

"How old are you?"

"Twenty-seven."

"That is young for shingles, but if you're under a lot of stress, it is possible to get them at any age. Are you under a lot of stress right now?"

"I don't know," I said. "The usual amount, I guess."

On the internet I find a Japanese myth that says if star-crossed lovers commit double suicide, they get reincarnated as twins, but I can't find a citation. I also can't figure out if the rebirth as twins is a punishment or a reward.

I saw Elena in 2-D before I saw her in 3-D. A flattened image. Alex had broken up with her girlfriend and invited me to an LGBT film festival, and we each chose a program to see. I picked a documentary about bisexual invisibility, and she chose a collection of lesbian short films. We just wanted to watch ourselves, I guess. Or we wanted to watch to see if we saw ourselves. Like standing in front of a filmic full-length mirror.

Elena's film was the first of the shorts program. It was an animated collage that mixed drawing, painting, photography, and film. The main character was a young girl growing up in a small Spanish town, with a squiggly line inside her belly that was giving her pain. She didn't have any friends, and her classmates called her *marimacho* (Spanish for *dyke*). This slur appeared as letters on the screen. It was a silent film, punctuated by moments of despair—when she wanted to play with the boys but wasn't allowed to, when she was made to wear a dress and didn't want to. Later, a series of black dots appeared on a white background and an invisible pen connected them, drawing the outline of her new adult body, curvy with breasts. Her short black hair sat on top of her head, like the dot of a Spanish upside-down exclamation point, saying, *¡I don't want this!*

Then, instead of a body, she was just an expectant face in a board game, the one where the object is to make pairs. A hand flipped up the tile next to her and it was a woman. They smiled at each other, thinking they'd won, but the match was no good, because the game only counted male-female couples.

Again, her animated form floated in the ether of a white background. Now she was boyish, in a hoodie and jeans. The squiggly line in her belly grew bigger and knottier and she tried to compact it with her hands to keep it inside. The sound of static filled the auditorium. Finally she reached deep into the mess of the knot and pulled it out like a splinter. The tangle was gone, her abdomen flat and empty. Everything was quiet, and I took my hands away from my ears. She watched the limp lines she'd pulled from inside her lying dead on the ground. Then they rose into the air and flew away like the birds we all drew as children. She turned and walked away from the camera, and I wanted to follow her. But it was over.

As the credits rolled, her name came up. Elena. That was it, no second name. Singular and self-assured. I applauded alongside everyone else in the darkness, acutely aware of the chair I was sitting on, of my hands touching each other. There was heat in my face. I had a crush on a cartoon. How silly was that? But really, this wasn't the first time I'd swooned for a two-dimensional heroine. As an eight-year-old, I'd watched *Who Framed Roger Rabbit* hundreds of times, just to see Jessica Rabbit slink around, pouting a Billie Holliday song. She'd turned me on.

"I am Elena and I come from Galicia," she said during the Q&A after the films. Her accent filled the auditorium, amplified by the microphone in her hand. I hung on the lisp she made when she said "Galicia." She sounded like a child.

Elena looked exactly like her avatar in the film, high-contrast and luminescent. Her pale skin glowed against her orange tank top, and a flounce of wavy black hair slouched off the top of her head, exposing her ears, her chin, her neck. My own ears were obscured behind the feathery shag that hung past my shoulders. I ached for her naked ears to touch mine, and the weight of my hair to evaporate.

Eric called from Maine. "You'll never guess who I was dancing with last night," he said.

"You were dancing?" I said. The last time he'd danced was at our wedding.

"Yeah, I love dancing now. Anyway, it was Janine Antoni! She's a visiting artist this summer and she came in last night. She pulled up in a convertible and offered me a ride to the costume party in the fresco barn. She was dressed like Frida Kahlo."

Janine Antoni was the performance artist I'd told Eric about when we first met, ten years earlier. I couldn't believe he was in her car, in the presence of that hair she had used to paint the floor. *It's not fair*, I thought. *It should be me in that car.* But did I want to be the driver or the passenger?

*I miss performing*, I'd often say. But maybe my definition of performance was too narrow. Maybe I was already performing without knowing it.

"Coupledom is performance art," says Phillips. "But how does one learn what to do together? How to be, once again, two bodies in public, consistently together, guardians of each other's shame . . ."

*There was a sort-of kissing orgy last night*, Eric wrote on iChat. *A bunch of us went skinny-dipping and everyone was making out.* I asked if the painter was involved. *No*, he said, *I was mostly making out with this other girl, but two guys tried to kiss me.*

I was excited by this turn of events. Maybe we're the same again, I thought.

*Now that I've tried it, I can definitely say it's not my thing.*

I sighed audibly as I sat alone in the living room.

More than anything, I was jealous of the skinny-dipping. I'd never skinny-dipped before, and I didn't know whether he had either. It was something that by age twenty-eight, I felt I should have done. We were more uneven than ever.

I sent Elena a message: *I really enjoyed your film at Outfest. Just wanted to let you know.*

She responded: *I'm in town for two weeks if you'd like to go for a coffee.*

I'd never felt an attraction to someone so androgynous, so much (as far as I knew from her film) a lesbian. She was someone Eric would certainly not be attracted to, so I wasn't sure how to talk about it with him, because I only felt comfortable discussing the desires that he shared. With any woman I was interested in, there was still the vague promise of a threesome, but if the woman wasn't interested in men, the possibility vanished, and with it my ability to be open about it. I thought in a perfect world that Eric and I would share everything—even lovers—and everything would be just and fair and same, and that sameness would keep us together. Elena didn't seem shareable, but Eric was three thousand miles away, so I didn't feel as much immediacy about his involvement.

I was surprised when I walked through the saloon doors of the bar to see Elena sitting with someone else. She rose to greet me and we kissed on each cheek as the Spanish do. She introduced the other woman as Laura. I wondered if Laura was her girlfriend, and if she'd brought her as a statement. I asked how they knew each other, and she said they'd met a few years ago, at a film festival in France.

"Laura had a very beautiful film there," Elena said. Laura blushed and deflected the compliment in a way that made it obvious she wished they were girlfriends. Elena complimented a film I'd made a few months earlier that she'd seen on my website, and I did as Laura had done. I turned the conversation to Galicia, and mentioned a trip Eric and I had taken to a nearby region to install a show for an artist he was assisting. "So you're married," she said.

"Yes. But he's away for three months at an art residency in Maine."

"What is Maine?" she asked, and Laura explained that it was a state on the East Coast.

I described the residency: fifty artists in the woods having sex with each other.

Elena smiled, amused. "So, is he?" she asked. I told her not sex, necessarily, but other things.

"We've had an open relationship for a while," I said, "but I only date women."

"Does he date men, then?" she asked, as others had before. They wanted an analogy, a direct correlation, something that approximated fairness.

Laura watched in silence as Elena described a girlfriend back in London. A fellow filmmaker, Russian, who was *a bit crazy*. "It's bumpy, our relationship," she said. "She wants it to be open, but I think I'm too jealous."

An hour or two later, after we'd parted ways, I got a text. *I'm sorry I brought Laura along. I shouldn't have. Can I see you again?*

The film Elena had complimented was something I'd made while Eric was in grad school. It was based on a correspondence I'd had with a boy in my high school French class. In other classes he was Mike, but in French he was Michel, soft and genderless to the ear. During our junior year, he studied abroad in France, and that was when I became interested in him—when he went away.

It was a short film, two minutes long, and consisted of overhead shots of a tabletop, messy with French books and stationery, close-ups of a pen scribbling on paper, maps of Paris and New York, and of me reading a letter while reclining in bed, my face obscured by the paper.

The voice-over was in French, like the letters we'd written. The narrator begins by saying that her French isn't very good but for the purpose of telling this story, it's necessary to use. She describes the arc of their pen-pal relationship, the way writing in French allowed them to say things they couldn't have said in English. *It was like wearing a mask; no one could see our eyes or our mouths. It was like our words belonged to someone else.*

The film ends with Michel's final letter, a confession of love written after he returns home and the two have drifted apart or, rather, maintained the distance they had while he was abroad.

*I suppose you'd like to know if I responded*, the narrator says. *I didn't. Like I said at the beginning: I don't speak French very well.*

Though cycling and ballet both had moments of feverish action, the sprints and petit allegros that pushed you to your physical and emotional limits, Eric and I were really endurance athletes. Our training prepared us for the multiday stage race, the three-act ballet. We'd learned not to dwell on the pain in the middle of one of these, because it would only grow; it would only slow you down. Those who worked through the pain did not get dropped from the peloton, did not get substituted by an understudy waiting in the wings.

So when we felt the particularly confusing pain of each other's growth, we did what came naturally to us. We encouraged each other, the way we had done with our teammates and fellow dancers. Our best friends and fiercest competition.

With text we clapped our hands mechanically and nodded our heads to the beat like cheerleaders. I told him about Elena, that she was Spanish, and liked my work. *That's great*, he said. He told me the painter had given him a hand job.

> Me: *Oooh!*
> Eric: *But it just . . .*
> Me: *No good?*
> Eric: *Yeah, it didn't work so well.*

I didn't know it was possible for a hand job not to work. He said it was partly that he'd been drinking too much, but mainly that her technique was not as good as mine. These compliments were key.

*Then we slept together on a yoga mat in my studio*, he said, and quickly clarified that he meant actual sleep, not sex. *You're cute*, I said. *You and your yoga mat.*

The following night Elena invited me to join her at a bar in Hollywood where her cousin, whom she was staying with, was DJing. When I found her inside, it was still early, and the bar was not that crowded. We ordered drinks and leaned our backs against the bar.

"So what are you doing here?" she said.

I didn't know what to say, so I recited the line back to her. "What are *you* doing here?"

"I'm here to watch my cousin DJ," she said.

"So am I," I said, lying.

She smiled, waiting for me to find my own line.

"And to see you," I said, taking a nervous sip of my drink. This satisfied her.

I could hardly bear standing beside her. I wanted to eat her up, as people do with babies. *I just wanna eat you up!* they say, leaning into cribs. But Elena was an adult. A woman, even if it was easy to mistake her for a man.

She resided so effortlessly between the masculine and the feminine. I wanted to follow her into that space because it didn't seem written.

Elena and I drove west. The moon was full, and part of Santa Monica had been shut down for an event on the beach.

There was trash everywhere. It was legal for that one night to drink in the streets. We didn't have alcohol with us, but we were already a bit drunk. We grasped each other's hands as we descended the stairs of the parking garage, turned our heads at the same time, and kissed. Her sour smokiness mixed with the saccharine sweet of my gum. We walked to the pier, past the throngs of people, and sat down in the sand. We were side by side, hip touching hip, shoulder connected to shoulder. She fit her head into the crook of my neck.

"You smell like books," she said.

"What kind of books?" I asked. There are two book smells. One is of old paper, slightly smoky, like the copy of *Catcher in the Rye* your dad read in high school and still has. The other smell is like cheese. There's something about the glue they used in kids' books, at least when I was young, that smelled like cheese to me. *Read me a cheesy book*, I'd demand at bedtime.

We sat on the sand and Elena positioned herself behind me, her legs straddling my legs, and wrapped her arms around my waist. In the light of the moon we saw the shapes of the waves coming toward us.

Eric told me he'd opened the door to his studio and a thin green snake had fallen from the doorjamb, skimming his face. Perhaps the snake was an omen, he wrote, because later, the painter had told him that she couldn't be physical with him anymore. She had a crumbling relationship at home and had begun to doubt it even more when she compared it to the relationship Eric seemed to have with me. *She can't handle that I'm "happy,"* Eric said.

The quotes scared me. Little eyelashes coyly batting around the word. An ugly truth prettied up by mascara.

> Me: *Are you?*
> Eric: *Of course. Those are her quotes.*
> Me: *Phew. I got a little worried.*
> Eric: *I couldn't be happier, and as disruptive as this is, I'm glad we're going through it.*

I agreed. I didn't know exactly what "this" was, but it felt like a passage we had to go through, a narrowing before the expansiveness beyond.

Offices with doors were rare in the open-plan creative workspace of the agency. It was a large warehouse with chic plywood half-cubicles that discouraged privacy. There were only four offices with actual doors and two had been empty since the account planners who occupied them had resigned. The offices remained empty because there was no one "senior" enough to merit them. Ethan asked if we could have the offices, and after a few days of deliberation, we were told yes.

That weekend, we went to the agency to move in. Ethan bought a faux leather daybed from the cheapo furniture company we'd first been hired to do ads for, and picked it up in the agency's SUV. We took down large pieces of paper hung on the walls by the previous occupants, displaying charts on market demographics and remnants of brainstorm sessions with phrases like NEW TASTE GRAZERS written in marker.

It was only after I helped Ethan move the desk away from the wall dividing our offices that I realized it was not solid. It was two giant doors painted white like the wall. I turned the doorknob but it was locked, so I ran out the front door of Ethan's office and into mine, unlocked the doorknob, and threw the doors open in a dramatic gesture.

"Hello!" I said.

"Hello!" he said.

We never closed those doors again. I propped them open with doorstops, and after just a few days, I'd forgotten they were there. The only reminder that it had ever been "offices" instead of just an office was the double-wide doorframe in the middle of the room, which was just tall enough to curl my fingertips over and hang from when I needed to stretch my back.

"Ooh," Ethan would say as I hung there, the bottom of my shirt creeping up over my midriff. I never felt he was being serious. It was more like he was performing the role of a straight man who'd say *ooh* to my bare midriff.

While the doors between us remained open, we closed the doors to the rest of the agency more and more frequently. Sometimes it was to keep the heat in. The building had many skylights, and once the sun went down, it got cold almost instantly. We kept the door closed so that the heat we built up couldn't escape into the polished concrete expanse of the rest of the office.

We could also shut out the noise while we tried to work. It got particularly noisy at five o'clock on Fridays, when people gathered at the kitchen island to get drunk on agency-provided beer and wine, until they moved on, either to their homes if they had children, or to a bar to eat happy-hour appetizers and get drunker if they didn't. Since Ethan didn't drink, we never joined them. If we were working late, I'd often venture out into the kitchen, pour myself a whiskey, and bring it back to our office.

"Just let me smell it," Ethan said one night.

I walked over to his desk and held the glass of whiskey under his nose. He closed his eyes and breathed in.

After the painter came a sculptor. The painter stopped talking to Eric altogether. We chatted for an hour about this and other dramas at the residency. I felt guilty about instant-messaging with Eric when I was supposed to be working, but Ethan chatted with his wife just as frequently, and they lived together.

"Do you have those headlines?" he asked without turning around. I remembered I'd promised him lines for a billboard, and told Eric I had to go.

*One last thing*, Eric said. The sculptor had asked if he had condoms in his studio.

*LOL*, I wrote back, though it did not correspond to actual laughter.

> Eric: *I don't know if I want to have sex with her or not.*
> Me: *You'll know in the moment. Just go with the flow.*
> Eric: *And you're ok with this?*

Instead of asking myself that question, I imagined Eric and I switching roles. In my head I told him I wanted to have sex with Elena, who was still in town for a few more days, and I gave the response I wanted to hear.

> Me: *I'm fine. I love you, and the most important thing is that I know you love me more than anyone else.*
> Eric: *I feel the same way.*
> Me: *And that we make it all work somehow.*

I saw the quotation bubble appear to show that he was typing something, but then it went away. I waited. It reappeared, then went away again.

Though I kept a journal during that summer, saved our emails and instant messages, I have no record of him telling me that he had sex with the sculptor. But I know they did. I recall him saying it wasn't great and he didn't plan to do it again. I find it odd that in all the correspondence I saved there is no confirmation of it after the fact. Only the foreplay.

The next night, Elena and I parked the car on Cahuenga and walked down the alley hand in hand. I was aware of her gait next to me and compared it to my own. We were in sync, but I felt as though I were hovering above the pavement, as if it were snow with a fresh layer of ice on top. I didn't want to crack the surface and make holes in it. I wanted to make myself light enough so that what was happening between us might go unnoticed by the universe.

In the bar, we sat in a booth and peeled the labels off our beers. "I want to be physical with you," she said.

I laughed. I wasn't sure if this was a too-literal translation from Spanish or just endearingly straightforward.

"Don't you?" she said.

We drove to her cousin's house where she was staying. The drive itself felt like a shrug. We said hello to the cousin and her husband and walked down the hall to his music studio, where they had put a mattress on the floor for Elena to sleep. We closed the door behind us and smiled. She laughed about the look they had given her, incredulous and admiring.

She lay back on the mattress and I stretched myself out on top of her. Her belt buckle dug into my waist, so I rocked back onto my knees and took it off her. I rubbed my face against her stomach, pulling on her underwear with my teeth.

I went running into the woods. I felt my way in, deeper still. I heard the sounds of animals panting and breathing, but I wasn't scared. I was an animal too, and I was running. I was using all four limbs. The smell of moss and mushrooms filled my nostrils as I ran over felled trees and trickling streams, skidding across great swaths of marshy grass, tripping, sliding on my belly through the mud, chin lifted so I could breathe.

We reached inside each other as though reaching into our mothers, trying to pull our long-lost twins out by the hand. *Come! Come!* Our voices echoed. *I cannot face this world without you. The air is dry. The mirrors are glass. I need your gaze to show me who I am.*

Eric and I reassured each other that we weren't being replaced. He made it clear that none of the women he'd been with compared to me. And since Elena was a woman and he was a man, the comparison was inherently more difficult.

We tried to shift our discussions away from the things we were doing with other people to the things we wanted to do to each other when he got home. He told me a story about a group of women taking turns biting one of the men on his birthday, and said it was incredibly hot.

I was surprised, because I remembered biting him once before, and being told I was too rough. It turned out the painter had bitten him too, and he'd liked it. *I want you to bite my arms and shoulders*, he said. *I want a mark there. Or two.*

Despite our talk of mark making, I worried that once we were face-to-face, we would fall back into a pattern of being careful with each other. An infinity mirror of delicacy. We tried to preempt it with dialogue.

> Me: *I want you to be a little less careful with me. That's all.*
> Eric: *I can be firm. This experience has opened me up to that.*

He said with the women at camp he'd felt more wild, and we agreed that we wanted that for us, a more dangerous kind of passion.

> Eric: *I felt like it was coming from me letting go and taking control.*

*Letting go* and *taking control* seemed at odds with each other, but it somehow made sense, that by letting go of control, you would be able to grab it.

On Elena's last night, I didn't want to sleep over at her cousin's because I had to be at work early. She asked to spend the night at my house and I obliged. I hadn't wanted to have sex with her in the bed I shared with Eric, but I figured sleeping was okay, even though for me it almost felt more intimate than sex. But Eric had slept with the painter, I reasoned, even if it had been on a yoga mat.

We didn't actually sleep; we stayed up all night talking. In the morning, I asked to photograph her with a film camera and she posed at my dining room table. She put her elbows on it and rested her chin in one hand. Her face was three-quarters to the camera, but her eyes looked directly into the lens. I took a long time focusing, but she didn't mind. She was calm and still, her eyes black and narrow.

The taxi arrived and we kissed goodbye, knowing it could be the last time. Our tongues moved slowly. The driver waited. The morning sunlight streamed down my street, magnified by the haze. She opened the door to the taxi and closed it, waving. I remained in the street until it was out of sight.

I walked back into the living room and it looked as it did on any morning, everything neat, all the chairs pushed into the table, except the one Elena had sat in. It was askew, open and casual, like uncrossed legs. Evidence of her absence.

I wanted to place myself in that absence, so I put the camera on a tripod and tried to remember exactly where I'd stood to take her photo. I'd been in the doorway of the bedroom, looking out into the living room, and I'd steadied myself against the doorjamb. I pressed the shutter and took a picture of the empty chair. I set up a tripod, wound the film, set the timer, and ran to the chair, posing as close as I could remember to how Elena had posed.

I dressed for work, and on my way there dropped off the film at the lab where I frequently took Eric's. Maribel was working, the stylish Mexican tomboy I often chatted with when I brought in Eric's film. She always had on colorful high-tops and wore her belt so the buckle rested over one hip, instead of over the fly. Now I realized how much she reminded me of Elena, or how much Elena reminded me of her. All three of us were the same height and weight—I could tell just by looking. I hoped she would be there when I returned later that day, but someone else was working when I picked up the negatives.

I'd been able to replicate the angle of the camera almost perfectly, so it looked as though Elena and I had sat for the portrait just minutes apart. Instead of both elbows, I only had one on the table, my other hand hanging at my side. The angle of my head was slightly different too. I'd cocked mine a bit more to the side, like a sad little dog tied up outside a store. The two photos were separated by a third of the empty chair. I emailed all three to her.

I also sent her something concrete: a book of my unfinished short stories. Some were first drafts, some only a first paragraph, some trailed off midsentence. Earlier that year, I'd had the idea to turn my inability to finish any of my writing into a conceptual art project. I'd printed a few copies and called it *Incomplet*.

A few days later, she emailed me a file: incomplete.mov. I didn't know if it was a reference to my project or not, whether she'd added the *e* on purpose or by accident. It turned out to be neither; the book hadn't yet made it to her in London.

The film started on black, with the sound of percussion. Light grew from the bottom left corner, filling the frame and revealing the picture I'd taken of the empty chair. It was hazier than the actual image—she had put a filter on it, which gave it the appearance of being on an old television. After a few beats of music, Elena's image materialized on the chair, like she was blood blooming through a bandage that had become saturated.

Elena's image disappeared and mine replaced it. Our legs were in the same place, and so were our torsos. The tiny shadow of an airplane arced across the wall behind me in the image, something she'd added in After Effects. My image disappeared from the chair, gone up in an invisible flame, leaving the empty space behind. I played it again and again, marveling at how the empty chair was no longer keeping us apart. Now it was a stage where we could perform our magic trick.

Elena and I sent each other selfies every day. Hers always looked bad-ass and boyish. She wore a baseball cap with the hood of her sweat-shirt pulled over it, peering out from under the protective awning of her garments. I mimicked these photos and felt the same low twinge when I took them as when I received them. "I like you *chico*," she said when she saw the photos. I loved that she could see me that way. A fellow tomboy.

Despite this symmetry, I felt off-balance. The deeper I went into my new relationship with her, the more I worried about losing my old one with Eric. I took different selfies and sent them to him. I played up my femininity, conjuring the aloof poutiness of a model. The photos he sent back were similar, but of course they were not the same. His blue eyes stared back at me, his blond hair, his maleness. The twinge I felt was higher. It was my heart.

I thought if Eric and I were clear like glass, we would not lose sight of each other. I strived for total transparency, total honesty, but it can be difficult to know if you are being totally honest. I gave him the closest thing I knew: *the blow-by-blow*, as they call it. It sounds like sex and war.

*I'm feeling a little obsessed with her*, I told him.

*I know*, he said. *I have to say I'm a little concerned.*

*Don't worry*, I said. *It doesn't change how I feel about you.*

*I just don't want you to leave me*, he said.

*I don't want to leave you, either.*

The residency was nearly over and Eric was surprised that almost no one had made any art. He'd thought it would be so productive, he said. While he hadn't made anything that involved code, he'd experimented with painting and video, and had been productive in other ways, we agreed.

Even if they weren't making art, I figured I would. I wanted to make a video art piece, mainly so I could watch it, the way I'd studied the tapes of my ballet performances over and over.

Watching myself on film was different from looking in a mirror. My mirror self was ever and always now, whereas the filmic me was caught in time. My filmic image seemed to have more autonomy; its movements on-screen were its own, unlike my mirror image, whose movements were just copies of mine.

Perhaps this is what it's like for a twin to see her sister from across the room at a party. To watch as she pours herself a glass of wine from a table of half-empty bottles and talks to a guy wearing a jean jacket with a hole in one elbow. She picks the skin on her thumb with her index finger, and then, finding that insufficient, pulls at the dry and ragged skin with her front teeth the way a dog pulls meat from a bone.

I put on a lacy pink bra with a rigid underwire and a matching thong I'd received for my bridal shower. They'd sat at the bottom of my lingerie drawer for the last four years, too obvious to wear under clothing and too obvious to wear without. I felt less sexy in things I was supposed to feel sexy in. I felt most sexy in anything that was the opposite: my father's old white undershirt, armpits yellowed from years of antiperspirant, and a pair of loose white pants I'd bought on sale that were two sizes too big. These clothes allowed me to focus on the way I felt in the world rather than how my body felt in the clothes.

Inspired by Elena's androgyny, I put on a pair of Eric's jeans and one of his white collared shirts over the bra and thong. I set the camera up and stood in front of the shiny white folding doors of our bedroom closet. I unbuttoned the collared shirt, taking care not to be seductive. I did this by devoting the perfect amount of time to each button. I did not linger; I did not tease. I removed the shirt and dropped it to the floor. I did the same thing with the pants, and then I turned around to remove the bra and underwear, standing naked, with my back to the camera.

I loaded the footage onto my computer, copied the clip, and reversed it. The movements seemed to happen of their own volition. Instead of my taking off the dress shirt and dropping it onto the floor, the shirt looked windblown as it leapt up from the ground and into my hand.

I recorded my voice speaking a mantra from *The Power of Now*, which both Eric and I had begun reading, and reversed that too. In reverse it became another language, something I knew had meaning but was unintelligible to my ear.

*Taht ma I ro, siht ma I erofeb, ma I.*

In the final video, I laid the reverse audio on top of the normal video. The gibberish mantra over the gender-bending nonstriptease striptease. I went from masculine to feminine to just human. Once I was naked, the video played in reverse, and the audio in the proper direction.

*I am, before I am this, or I am that.*

It looped endlessly, the image and language in opposition.

After meeting Elena, I spent a lot of time looking at Tumblr sites that collected photos of sexy androgynous people. Male models with long hair and high cheekbones. Short-haired girls with pretty faces and flat chests. It excited me to see the roles they had available to themselves, and the roles available to me in their presence.

Back in the day, if they suspected you were dead, they'd put a mirror in front of your mouth, and if you fogged it up, they knew you were still alive.

When I cut my hair short like Elena's and dressed in boyish clothes, it was like seeing her when I looked in the mirror. I felt alive.

"I like you *chico*," I said to the mirror, giving voice to a part of myself that had long been silent.

Ballerinas are silent. And they aren't tomboys. The ballerina is the archetype of femininity: beautiful and controlled. Long hair coiled on top of the head, a tutu whose bodice is boned like a corset and whose skirt shows the legs, unblemished beneath pale pink tights, accented with satin shoes and ribbons. I was finally free of all that.

In high school, Mr. Chang taught the ballet class called Partnering. His teaching style reminded me of the gymnastics coaches I saw on the Olympics. It was firm and physical, but somehow playful—a push here, a swat there—and rougher than Americans are comfortable with. Mr. Chang's accent made him difficult for me to understand. The commands he barked sounded like proverbs. "Don't be door. Be window." He'd lightly slap our chins away if we looked at our reflections. "Don't see mirror!" He wanted us to look at our partners, the boys who manipulated and spun us like tops. It was almost impossible to avoid looking at the mirror, since it extended the length of the studio, from floor to ceiling. Nonetheless we were expected to ignore ourselves.

Once we were onstage, we wouldn't be able to peek at the mirror, so we might as well learn how these moves felt instead of how they looked. Later, feeling was all we would have. And I did know that onstage, when you weren't looking at yourself, dancing could be truly transcendent. That was when the emotion happened. It was difficult to emote while watching yourself emoting.

That summer, I logged countless hours in front of my computer, emailing, instant messaging, and video chatting with both Eric and Elena. During these video chats, I tried not to look at myself in the small square at the bottom corner of the video chat window. I tried to look into the face of the person I was talking to, but I often ended up directing my conversation at myself. Instead of seeing them, I saw my reflection. I tipped the screen back and forth, trying to find a flattering angle. There wasn't one.

When Eric returned from the wilds of the summer, I picked him up at the airport. It was strange to be in a car again, he said, as we sat in traffic for nearly twenty minutes just trying to exit the terminals at LAX. He hadn't been behind the wheel for the entire summer, and had only been in a car once or twice.

I'd warned him that I'd cut my hair, so he wouldn't be surprised that it was the same length as his. Even though I'd been reveling in the ability to inhabit my more masculine self, I'd sent him pictures of me in lip gloss and a nautical striped shirt, my head tilted at pretty angles, styling myself into a Godardian gamine.

It was clear that we were no longer the same two people who had driven to the airport three months earlier, and yet here we were, side by side, sharing the same air. Later, he'd tell me he couldn't breathe that air. He was having a panic attack—his first, so he didn't know what was happening. He kept it hidden so I had no idea. He was a good performer, my twin. Like a beautiful dancer, he didn't let the audience know he was in pain.

In many cultures, seeing a person's doppelgänger is bad luck. It means they might be in danger or become ill. Seeing your own doppelgänger is worse. An omen of death.

Despite our talk of being less careful with each other, Eric and I mostly went back to our old routines. On weekends, we shared an order of French toast at the café up the street. We went to art openings and museum shows. We revisited an old hobby and made it new. Fixed-gear and single-speed bikes had become popular and I was attracted to their style, the colorful vintage road-bike frames like the one my dad had ridden all those years, retrofit with fewer gears and narrow, flat handlebars. Eric was happy I was finally riding a bike.

We spent a lot of time working on our bikes that year, tweaking them, adding components. Different grips, colorful anodized aluminum cranksets, chains and wheels ordered from Japan. We did it together but we made them our own. Eric used clipless pedals, but I wore my regular shoes and slipped into toe clips, little cages that didn't lock. Because of this, I almost never fell.

I loved the freedom of it, skirting past traffic, weaving between cars. I rode my bike to work every day. It only took fifteen minutes. It was easier to share one car now that we had other forms of transportation. We didn't have to do everything together or leave each other stranded anymore.

Eric got a studio with someone from the residency and was home less often. Still, I had to hide the fact that I was in constant contact with Elena. It wasn't that difficult. Even when Eric was home, we were always both on our computers. But I know he could sense I was somewhere else, existing in limbo.

In addition to our endless Skype chat and selfies that detailed the minutiae of our day, Elena and I sent pictures of the full moon, and told each other when our periods arrived each month. They were short notes in both cases—with the moon, it was just the subject line, *La Luna*, and a photo of the moon in the body of the email. With the period, it was the word *sangrando* (bleeding), if we were in the middle of it, or *la sangre viene* (the blood comes), if it was imminent. I liked this phrase. *The blood comes. The blood cometh.* It felt grand and Shakespearean, public and important, instead of the way I used to see my period. Nagging and personal.

This cycle of bleeding had always seemed a nuisance to me. I felt that men were lucky they didn't have to endure it. When I exercised too much or ate too little and my period stopped for a few months, I saw it as a blessing. I had transcended this curse of femininity.

I was intrigued by Elena's embrace of her period and the way she encouraged mine. It had been her masculine exterior that had attracted me in the first place, but even with my new boyish look, she was making me see the particular magic, the cosmic importance, of being female. I decided to devote myself to worshipping these monthly occurrences with her.

Ethan and I each bought deep V-neck T-shirts, which were popular for men that season. They were so deep they reached the bottom of our sternums and touched the pointy piece of cartilage called the xiphoid process, a body part I feared. When we learned CPR in high school, they warned us not to push on the xiphoid process, saying it could break off, puncture various organs, and cause internal hemorrhaging.

When I wore the V-neck with my short hair and baggy jeans, I felt like a pretty boy.

The deep V-neck drew attention to our nipples, mine and Ethan's. They were hidden away, just inches from the diagonal band of ribbed jersey, and they frequently hardened under the air-conditioning that was pumped into our office. One day I saw him put on a thin black nylon jacket, so thin it could fold up into the size of a wallet. I asked where he got it and he told me.

"You should get one," he said. "Mine is a small, but they had an extra-small too." I went to the store at lunchtime and bought one. Back at the office, we zipped them up in sync and our nipples relaxed.

Even though we closed the doors of our office to keep the heat in, they did not give us full privacy. The doors were glass, and from the outside our uniforms must have given the appearance of a united front, an impenetrable fortress of us-ness. But from the inside, where our body heat commingled, and where we spent many rambling hours concepting, but also digressing into conversations about our relationships, our sex lives, and bathroom habits, the zippers on our identical jackets and the buttons on our identical jeans kept our bodies to ourselves.

That winter, the agency sent Ethan and me to Australia for three weeks. We were shooting a series of commercials there because the Australian dollar was weak, and we could get more for our money. More special effects, nonunion actors, and two tons of candy sprinkles we made fall from the sky like rain to illustrate the coverage of our client's internet signal. We were accompanied by an account manager and a producer, and we got to fly business class and stay in a hotel right on the water. My room was two levels, and larger than my apartment in LA.

A wall was all that separated us. In the wall was a door, and the door had a lock, and we kept it locked. When we needed to work on something, we'd meet downstairs at the restaurant or bar, or go out for a walk to find a coffee shop nearby. He didn't even peek his head into my room when he came by to pick me up. I always tried to look into his, to see what he left on the floor, on chairs, how he lived in a space that looked exactly the same as mine.

It was a relief to not have to hide my communication with Elena from Eric. I was nine hours ahead of Elena and seventeen ahead of Eric, and because of that our chats never conflicted. Elena was still seeing the Russian, but they didn't live together, so it was easy for her to carry on our constant conversation.

In the morning on my first day, I wrote to her on Skype before she went to bed. *I'm off to work at a café*, I said.

*Come mucho*, she typed, and I almost mistook the Spanish word *come* for the English one.

I thought about the first time she saw me naked. "You're so esskinny," she had said, as we lay side by side in her cousin's bed and she drew her finger across the canyon of my abdomen, up the rim of my hip bone.

*Ya comí la cena y estoy taaaaaan llena*, she typed. I knew that she was talking about herself as a whole, that she was so full, not just her stomach. In Spanish it is *llena* for her, and *lleno* for her stomach, because *el estómago* is masculine. She hadn't needed to modify *esskinny* for me because it's not a Spanish word. In English, we don't care about the gender of words. Just bodies.

Ethan and I couldn't stand the thought of going three weeks without riding our bikes, and since work was paying for it, we'd bought airline cases and brought them to Sydney. Still slightly jet-lagged, we set out in search of a café the production company had recommended for breakfast.

Riding in a city is difficult. Riding in a city you don't know is even more so, and riding in a city where they drive on the other side of the road was a challenge we hadn't anticipated. We arrived at the café after a harrowing ride, our V-neck T-shirts drenched in sweat from the Southern Hemisphere November sun. We hadn't spoken during the ride. I'd just followed him and tried not to die.

"Whoa," I said, as I locked my bike to a parking meter.

"I know," he agreed. "That was insane."

We hugged, and something about it felt different. It was the same hug we frequently exchanged, when things were going badly at work, or when we pulled up in front of Swingers on a Monday morning to work over breakfast, but imbedded in it was the intimacy and danger of traveling together in a foreign country. That was something I'd only done with my husband.

We ordered a celebratory breakfast, grateful for our expense account, and for not having gotten ourselves killed on our bikes. The spell was broken, and he was once again just my colleague, my annoying little brother. I ate the toast he'd slathered with Vegemite and abandoned after I told him he should probably taste it first to see if he liked it.

Eight hours later, I found an email in my inbox. It was a photo of Elena's breakfast, shot from above. A single fried egg on a piece of toast. The bubbly white was free-form and wild within the right angles of the toast, and in the center of it all were two perfect yolks, next to each other. They stared back at me, a pair of eyes, a pair of breasts, two marigold suns. She was having twins for breakfast.

During our second week in Sydney, Eric went to Art Basel in Miami with friends from the residency. Like the residency, Art Basel had a debauched reputation, but with more collectors than artists, more swimming pools than lakes, more cocaine than whiskey. The first night, he'd gotten into a private party where a band we both loved performed for a couple of hundred people. The second night, he'd made out with a painter who'd just gotten out of a long-term relationship with a famous film director.

On the third night, he called and said, "We're going to Dubai! I just won a raffle!" I didn't understand. Music and street noise made it hard to hear his voice. "An all-expenses-paid trip for two to the art fair in Dubai!"

I couldn't recall ever having won a raffle, and certainly not for something so extravagant. I was jealous of his luck until I realized he was asking me to come along. By *we* he meant us. The luck was ours.

At the end of a long day of shooting, Ethan and I got an email saying the hamburger client had killed a spot they'd previously approved, and we needed to come up with new ideas by the end of the LA business day. We'd already had dinner, and it was late, so Ethan invited me to his room to work.

I got a cocktail from the hotel bar and took it back to his room. I settled on the carpet, leaning against an upholstered chair while Ethan sat back against the pillows at the headboard of the unmade bed. This was how it happened, that coworkers began affairs with each other. I wondered whether we would have considered it a long time ago if Ethan had been single, in the office late at night after everyone had gone home. Work relationships were the opposite of most romances. Instead of starting out passionately and becoming companionate, they work in reverse. The more you're around the coworker, the more you flirt with them or fantasize about them, mostly out of boredom or necessity. I'd often wondered whether being in a relationship with someone who was bisexual, like Ethan, would have felt different than being in a relationship with Eric. Or Elena, even.

I took a drink of my Manhattan and it tasted strange. The bartender had asked if I wanted it dry, sweet, or perfect. No one had ever asked me how I wanted my Manhattan. "I guess perfect," I said. "That'd be sort of right down the middle, right?"

He said it would be.

I didn't know he meant sweet and dry vermouth. You never put dry vermouth in a Manhattan, that much I knew for sure. It tasted terrible but I drank it anyway.

Ethan and I pitched each other ideas for commercials. We prefaced every idea with *This may be stupid, but* . . . Eventually we'd written enough scripts that we decided we could be done.

"What's Eric up to?" he asked.

"He's at this art thing in Miami," I said, "making out with some girl, and sharing a cheap hotel room with ten other people. It's like spring break."

"Aren't you jealous?" he said. "I am!" He'd said that about the residency as well, and the open relationship.

I was, of course, but I wouldn't admit it. I didn't want to be a cliché character. I was still determined to transcend the role of the Average Woman, the Jealous Woman. "It's not like I'm not having fun too," I said, and shrugged.

When I was done with my Manhattan, I took a bite of an apricot I'd bought at the grocery store earlier in the week. I'd never had a fresh apricot before—I was used to seeing them dried like leather or embalmed in jam. Sadly, it was bland and boring, neither sweet nor bitter. I guess I could say it was perfect too, though it didn't look it. One side had bruises, and I wondered if I'd made them. Normally I would have thrown it away, but that night, I decided to eat it, bruises and all. I'd had it with so-called perfection.

They were the best bites of any fruit I'd ever had. I vowed never again to avoid the hurt parts of things.

"I got into the Whitney," Eric told me when we were back in LA. A strange phrase without context. He meant the Whitney Independent Study Program, a one-year residency for artists, curators, and art historians, affiliated with the Whitney Museum of American Art in New York.

The museum is usually called the Whitney, the way the Metropolitan Museum of Art is the Met, but it's funny to say *the* before what is typically a woman's first name. The Whitney, as though it's a person, but a person so important she requires *the* before her name to differentiate her from all other Whitneys. Not just any Whitney. *The* Whitney.

"They only accept twelve people a year," he said. "What should I do?"

"You should go," I said. I didn't say *we*. He agreed.

I'd just gotten a raise and promotion at work. Ethan and I were creative directors now, and I didn't want to have to start all over again at an agency in New York. I'd already uprooted myself twice for Eric, and I'd been happy to do it. This time I wanted to stay put and grow. I wanted to branch out. The three months we'd spent apart in the summer while he was in Maine felt like just the beginning. I needed the distance. Without it, I felt too enmeshed in the fabric of our relationship. It had been the backdrop to my entire world for so long.

We agreed it could be good for us, that we could use the time apart to grow, but we refused to call it a *separation*. *We'll just live separately for a year*, we said, like it was nothing.

Whenever Eric had success, I felt particularly aware of the success I hadn't had. I hadn't danced the part of Odette/Odile. I hadn't completed my short story collection. I'd made a short film, but not a feature.

I think I believed there was a finite amount of success any couple could have at any given moment. If Eric was having a lot of success, the amount available to me was diminished, the same way the more viable twin fetus crowds out the weaker one.

Eric was more viable now. I feared his success would flatten me.

I also wanted Eric to go to the Whitney because I wanted to go to the Elena. The Whitney had chosen him, and I felt special when I was with her, that she had chosen me.

But I couldn't go to the Elena, not for any long period of time, anyway. I had a full-time job, and if Eric was going to live in New York for a year, we were going to double our expenses, and it would be up to me to keep our joint bank account full. Elena would have to come to me.

Eric agreed to this, that she could stay with me for the first two weeks he was gone, to ease the transition. Perhaps he felt guilty about the growth he was undergoing, about leaving me behind.

In the waning months before Eric's departure, we went on the free trip to Dubai. I researched social codes for travelers, and learned that foreign women did not have to cover their heads, but that modest dress was required. Knowing that our hotel also featured a water park called Wild Wadi, I purchased the first one-piece bathing suit I'd bought in years. *Public displays of affection are strictly prohibited*, one website said, *even between a husband and wife.*

Though other Western women had their heads uncovered, I was the only woman with short hair. This was certainly not a good place to be a gay person, I assumed, so I was surprised, when we visited the gold souk, the spice souk, the fish market, and the canals, to see Middle Eastern men holding hands with each other. *Is Dubai a Middle East gay haven?* I wondered. I knew it was more lax than some of its neighbors, allowing alcohol to be served in hotels to attract foreign tourism.

Since the time zone was exactly twelve hours ahead of Los Angeles, our circadian rhythms were completely off for the four days we were there. Eric had always been a better sleeper than I was, but even he was struggling. At night, he lay in bed and tried to sleep, but I stayed up, dimming my computer screen so as not to disturb him, and messaged Elena photos we'd taken that day. I'm sure he knew what I was doing, but he said nothing. We were both delirious.

I googled "men holding hands in Dubai" and found a number of images to confirm what I'd seen that day. I also found an article in the *New York Times* with an image of George W. Bush holding hands with Crown Prince Abdullah of Saudi Arabia.

"Americans may raise an eyebrow at men holding hands, but in the Arab world, affection among men is common, and without sexual connotation," the article said. "Holding hands is the warmest expression of affection between men. It's a sign of solidarity and kinship."

I whispered Eric's name in the dark to tell him my discovery, but he didn't answer.

Since our free flight home from Dubai required a stop in London, we decided to spend our own money to stop first in Paris for three days and take the Chunnel to London to catch our plane home.

I was looking forward to revisiting the place of our honeymoon, to speak French and sit in cafés, but I couldn't bear the thought of stopping in London without seeing Elena. It had been a year of daily communication and I wanted more than just words and images. I wanted to feel and touch her to know she was real, to locate her in her own space.

Eric begrudgingly agreed to spend two extra nights in London before returning to LA. I spent a lot of time looking for an affordable hotel near the art galleries I hoped would distract him while I was with Elena. I thought if the hotel was comfortable enough, perhaps he wouldn't mind if I spent one of the nights with her.

On our last evening in Paris, we took a bottle of wine down to the Seine and drank. I told him that I wanted him and Elena to meet while we were in London. I didn't want to feel I was hiding one from the other.

"I'll meet her," he said. "But if I'm being honest with myself, I don't want you to stay with her."

I didn't want to push my luck. "Okay," I said. "Let's see how it goes."

It seemed strange that when we were in the same city, it didn't matter what I did with someone else, so long as Eric and I spent the night together. Like my arrangement with Jimena. On some level, I did understand; at night there's little to distract you from your thoughts and worries, and knowing someone is not there is much more disturbing when they are close than when they are far away. This was why it had been easier while he was at the residency, and why I looked forward to the time when we'd be in different cities.

In the morning we took the train under the English Channel. We both slept most of the way, which made it easy not to talk about our plans. A few hours later we checked into the hotel, and I was relieved at how lovely it was. In the room, Eric sat on a chair instead of the bed while I stood.

"So, what should I do?" I said, even though I knew what he wanted. "She's been expecting me to stay and I feel bad changing my plans."

"You know how I feel," he said, "but you can do what you want."

"I kind of want to go."

"Then go," he said.

"Are you sure?"

"Yes."

I asked again, emphasizing the word *sure*. He gave me the same answer. I asked again and again, hoping that at some point I'd hear *no*, but I didn't. Instead, each time I heard *yes*, I tried to convince myself that it meant something different.

*Yes, I'm okay spending the night alone while you have sex with your lover.*

*Yes, I'm okay with you having a relationship with someone else.*

*Yes, I will stay married to you even though it is hurting me.*

I put a change of underwear in my purse and walked out the door. *What if this is it?* I thought, replaying the image of my hand, stuffing the pair of black cotton underwear into my bag. *What if this is the final gesture of our relationship?* I felt helpless at its improvisational quality. I hadn't planned it. I hadn't choreographed it. It felt undignified.

A blush of shame colored my face while my feet moved on the sidewalk in time to my heart. Like the aggressive thumping of a timpani, it emanated from my orchestra pit and filled the theater of my body. It had never beat this hard before, not after a ballet performance, not even a solo.

I had been pushing Eric for so long. Pushing, but also pulling away. I'd tested his patience, his love, his loyalty and self-respect, and I could sense, without him saying so, that he was making a vow to himself that this would be the last time he just stayed.

The psychoanalyst D. W. Winnicott says that a child must destroy her mother and the mother must survive that destruction in order for them to have a healthy relationship.

A vanished twin does not survive its sibling's destruction. It disappears. I wondered if Eric would do the same.

I descended into the Underground and imagined Elena's flat. I knew she lived on the top floor of a tall building in one of the South London tower blocks called *council estates*. I had seen the view from her window many times, in the photographs and time-lapse videos she'd sent me, but I wanted to see it for myself. To feel the vertigo.

Elena was waiting as I came up the escalator at her tube stop. "Call him," she said. "Let him know you're here and okay."

I was surprised that he answered and even more surprised at his tone. It seemed lighter than I'd expected, but maybe I had a way of filtering out the things I didn't want to hear. I said I would return the next day, so we could spend our last night together at the hotel. I wouldn't want to miss the train to Heathrow, I joked. "I should hope not," he said.

I don't remember sex with Elena, though I know we had it. What I do remember are the creaking sounds her sofa made. We pictured ourselves on a sailboat, adrift at sea—the creaks were the rigging; the ropes groaning under the tensions. We lay side by side, rocking back and forth, playing the sofa like an instrument while she recorded the sounds on a device she kept in her bag, to use for animations.

In the evening we took a bath, and I let her shave my legs. She did not cut me.

The next morning I texted Eric to let him know when I'd be back and asked again if he would meet Elena. He agreed. She suggested a dive bar that was a short walk from our hotel.

We arrived first and sat inside on the dirty sofas. I was nervous. I wanted so badly for him to like her and bless our relationship, as impossible as I knew that might be.

Elena was nervous too, and went outside to smoke. She'd already smoked three spliffs that day, to calm her nerves, I assumed, but then I realized I didn't really know how much she smoked when she was in Europe and hash was readily available. I had only known her vacation self: the traveler, the guest.

I began to worry that she and Eric would meet outside, but she returned to the sofa moments before he came through the front door. I walked to meet him, and we hugged and kissed quickly on the lips. Elena appeared at my side, and I introduced them. Moments later, a friend of hers also appeared. She hadn't mentioned this invitation, and it reminded me of how she'd brought a friend the first time she met me. She needed a buffer, I realized. Perhaps she was not as confident as I'd thought.

We walked next door for dinner. Everyone was cordial, but no one felt the need to linger once we were finished. When we parted ways, Eric suggested we walk Elena to the tube—a gesture that surprised me.

"Well?" I asked, as soon as she had disappeared down the stairs at the station. "What do you think?"

He remarked on how mellow she was (probably the hash), how soft-spoken. He said he was glad they had met, and that he was somehow less worried about her than he'd been when she was just an image or an idea.

I felt a desire I'd never felt before, rooted in gratitude and bewilderment. We went directly to bed when we got home. It was different from our normal routine, more modern than ballet. Martha Graham and Merce Cunningham. I felt beautiful with my concave back and bent legs. No pristine satin between us, no tights, just bare feet. I didn't feel like I was doing him a favor. I wanted to honor his desires because he was still there after I'd pursued mine.

Later, he told me that I was more giving and less inhibited than I'd ever been. He remembered every dirty thing I said that night.

It took him longer to tell me that what he remembers most from the trip is that he was so distraught while wandering around London in the grip of an icy panic that he stepped off a curb looking the wrong direction and was nearly hit by a double-decker bus. He said it was the closest he'd ever come to death.

ACT THREE

# ACT THREE

I picked up *A Lover's Discourse* from one of the front tables at a bookstore in LA. It was the first book of fragments I'd read, and I was moved by the way these bits of wisdom added up to such a profound and complete description of the experience of being in love.

Barthes sees only two possible roles in a love relationship: the beloved (the one who leaves) and the lover (the one who awaits the other's return).

I knew how to be the one who left. My twin in the womb. Ballet. Eric.

But I was tired of being the beloved. The lover seemed like a better role. A lover can yearn. And without yearning, there is no satisfaction in the eventual connection, the grasp of the hand. If I wanted to be the lover, I'd need to put down roots and be still, like a plant.

That's what I did when Eric moved to New York for the Whitney. I grew roots right down through the carpet of our second-floor apartment, to the carport and the concrete below. It wasn't easy, though. I couldn't sleep the night before. I had heart palpitations as I drove him to the airport, stage fright. We wore our own clothes, but we had traded costumes. *In this evening's performance*, a voice over a loudspeaker said to an audience sitting quietly in their theater seats, *the role of the beloved will be played by Eric.*

It was then that I became the lover.

I had to work while Elena was visiting, but she was happy to stay home and cook for me. She wanted to be my housewife, she said. I was surprised to hear her use that phrase.

We instant-messaged while I was at work. *I tried on your white trousers and your black dress*, she wrote, adding a blushing-face emoticon. She said she liked them. I liked that she was curious about being me.

She didn't mind when I spoke to Eric on the phone. She knew it was important for me to try to keep the balance. She spoke to her girlfriend occasionally on Skype, but never when I was around. Her girlfriend was seeing someone else in London and things were falling apart.

In the mornings, she rode Eric's bike with me to work, and interviewed the day laborers who waited on the street corner near my office. She was thinking about her next film.

We'd kiss quickly before I got to the parking lot. I didn't want my colleagues to think I was cheating on Eric. No one except Ethan knew about the open relationship.

Her cousin was getting married up in the sequoias, so we took a road trip there. In the woods, we took hundreds of photographs of ourselves. I'm hard-pressed to tell who is who in the photos we took of each other from behind, standing on a rock, overlooking some rapids. Topless in our underwear, our short hair dark with river water.

We went to her cousin's wedding dressed very much alike: she in a black tank top and pants, me in a black dress and boots. We untagged ourselves when photos were posted online.

She decided to extend her trip for a third week and I could tell Eric was not pleased when I told him on the phone.

I'd heard immersion was the best way to learn a language, so while she was staying with me, I'd asked that she speak only Spanish. But it wasn't just language. I wanted to immerse myself in her.

We conversed in rudimentary sentences, and I'd watch her mouth and mimic her, making *th* sounds for *c*'s and *z*'s as they do in Spain, even though it felt wrong, like a speech impediment. I watched her face as I spoke, to see whether the words I chose made sense, changing them midstream if her eyes squinted or she opened her mouth to correct me. When she spoke too quickly, her Spanish sounded like gibberish, and nothing in her face helped me decode it. I'd follow her eyeline to a chair, or to my wristwatch sitting on the bedside table, trying to find meaning in the objects she settled on.

"Something about my watch?"

"I'm not always talking about what I'm looking at," she'd say.

The words snapped me like a rubber band. She was getting impatient with me, her student. And I was impatient too. I wanted our needs to be magically understood and met. I wanted us to be fluent in each other.

In *The Psychology of Twinship*, the psychologist Ricardo Ainslie says that our desire for simple, automatic relationships, for sameness, is a desire to return to the relationship we had with our mother in the womb. He calls it symbiotic return.

"It's what we all look for in partners . . . [we] wish to return to a symbiotic relationship—that is, a relationship characterized by a lack of self-other differentiation in which one's needs are magically understood and met."

The original symbiotic relationship is between mother and child, but Ainslie suggests that, with twins, it can also be between baby and baby.

"There's an experience of self and other as being one . . . A complete closeness. A sense of immersion in another person that feels whole and complete and almost ideally satisfying."

*Almost* ideally satisfying. This troubles me. If diving headfirst into the pool of another person and sinking deep to their depths can yield only an "almost ideal" satisfaction, where can you find something total and absolute?

Elena smoked a lot. In the States she rolled cigarettes with tobacco and pot, since she couldn't get hash. She always had rolling papers close at hand. Tiny slips of paper; delicate leaves in her pockets, her bag, her mouth. *Paperwhites*, I thought.

After we met, I'd been struck with the idea that I would write a novella inspired by our relationship, and rolling papers seemed like the perfect thing to write it on. They were sturdy enough to be carried around, but easily disintegrated by fire or saliva. They invited a kind of telling I might not have been capable of on more permanent stock. I told Elena I would give the novella to her to smoke, and then there would be no remnant of it. It would become part of her the way she'd become part of me.

When Eric and I were in Paris before he'd left for New York, I'd looked for an ashtray to use for my project, because they are nearly impossible to find in the States. Initially my search hadn't yielded anything but souvenir ashtrays with the French flag or a picture of the Eiffel Tower. Then one afternoon, when Eric and I returned to our rented flat, I noticed that the shop next door sold an array of white ceramic objects in every shape and size: salt and pepper shakers, teacups, platters, tart pans, ramekins, tiny pitchers for cream.

Inside I found the perfect ashtray—square and pure white, with space to rest one cigarette on each side. Eric bought a soap dish. It was also white and unblemished. A quiet object. He said he'd been looking for one for some time.

They were like fraternal twins, the soap dish and the ashtray. One a cradle for cigarettes—dirty, sexual objects—and the other for soap—a cleansing tool, a milky weapon of erasure. Maybe Eric and I subconsciously meant to buy these gifts for each other, but instead bought them for ourselves.

As I write it now, it is difficult for me to see the word *ashtray* and not read it as *astray*.

"*Tengo que decirte*," she said one night. *I have to tell you.* She paused, waiting for me to prod her along. I could sense in the hush of her voice what she wanted to tell me.

"*Que?*" I said.

"*Que te quiero.*"

I was confused by this phrase. I knew that *querer* was *to want*. Was she telling me she wanted me? No, she said, she was telling me that she loved me.

I didn't want to tell her that I loved her. That was something I told Eric and I wanted to keep it sacred. But *te quiero* was different, I reasoned. The fact that I didn't quite grasp its meaning or proper usage helped. "*Te quiero también*," I said.

Elena and I had matching bruises. They were created one night in bed toward the end of her three-week stay. We had been reading when I asked if she would bite me on the arm, remembering Eric's story from camp.

"Like, how?" she said.

"Like, just a little," I said.

We put our books aside. I lay on my back and she propped herself up on her elbow and approached my shoulder. As her mouth covered my deltoid, I felt her teeth touch my skin, digging in lightly. She hesitated.

"More," I said. "More. More."

Her mouth was open wide like a snake. She began to clamp down on my arm so slowly I almost couldn't feel her jaw moving. I could not believe her patience.

"More," I said when I thought I felt her stop.

She bit down harder, and I waited for the pain I was expecting: a pinching, a burning. But the pain I felt was a kind of claustrophobia. Like her mouth was something I needed to get out of. Instead of saying "Stop," I pushed her forehead away, and she pulled back, saliva hanging from her mouth in strings, like a vampire.

"No one has ever let me do that to them," she said.

I smiled. "Let me do it to you."

I tried to mimic her slowness. It was difficult. She lasted about the same amount of time under my teeth as I had under hers before she pulled her arm away. Our pain thresholds were on par. I felt relieved by the knowledge that I'd never give her more pain than she could take, as long as I never gave her more pain than I could take myself.

We both got bruises from the biting. They were big round circles, like rings around invisible planets located beneath our skin. They were blue at first, then purple, then yellow, like old newspapers.

A few days later, she went back to London. When I dropped her off at the airport, we both wore long-sleeved shirts to cover our marks. I didn't want people thinking I'd been beaten.

I asked an employee at the health food store how to make the bruises fade more quickly. She suggested arnica, and it worked. I was going to Brooklyn to visit Eric in a few days, and I didn't want him to see the traces of how I'd let Elena hurt me. He and I had never gotten around to biting each other, and I worried the marks I'd let her give me would hurt him too much.

I was excited to see Eric, desperate to reconnect and prove to myself that everything was okay. I tried to kiss him in public but he didn't want to be affectionate. This surprised me, because when we spoke on the phone, he seemed to miss me so much. But that was when Elena was staying with me, when I wasn't as available as I normally made myself. I tried not to let his resistance to public displays of affection worry me. Maybe I was used to being with Elena, the way you can't keep your hands off someone when you're first together. It was part of the NRE, as I had read it was called in polyamory circles: new relationship energy.

Eric had NRE too, for his new city. It was so much easier to socialize in New York, he said. You could make friends anywhere, even on the train. His was the coolest up-and-coming neighborhood in Brooklyn, and everyone was young, attractive, artsy, bookish. For years, we had longed to live on the hipper Eastside of LA where many of our friends lived, but we were pragmatists. We didn't want to commute to the Westside for work and school, and could afford not to. I was jealous of his new situation but also defensive about my Los Angeles, where I'd chosen to remain.

I showed Eric pictures of Elena and my time in LA, touristy photos of scenic overlooks and city streets but also domestic tableaus of
breakfasts, unmade beds, the contents of her pockets laid out on top
of the dresser. I didn't mean this to be hurtful. Keeping this evidence
only for myself seemed secretive and selfish. Surely the guilt I felt was
a signal that what I was doing was wrong. But instead of stopping, I
decided to share, hoping that lifting the cloak of secrecy would make
it right somehow.

I thought there was an altruism to my sharing—that it would help
him feel included. But it only repelled him. I had turned our magnet
around.

I was wearing Elena's clothes. Tight, low-slung gray jeans from the men's section that exposed the waistband of my underwear when I lifted the baggy shirt over my head as I changed my clothes before we went to dinner the first night.

"Is that what you're wearing?" he asked.

"Is there a problem? It's basically the same thing you're wearing."

"That's the problem," he said.

"Fine. I'll change," I said. But I didn't want to change. Neither did he.

Fall was turning to winter in New York and Eric felt exposed. Having lived in LA for so long, he didn't have any warm clothes, so we went to a Scandinavian clothing store near his studio where he'd seen a wool jacket he wanted my opinion on. I liked it. I'd only seen Eric in snow jackets in Colorado, and the wool peacoat transformed him into someone else. A steely, Nordic European.

In the women's section of the store, a modest black dress caught my eye. Sensible cotton with a slight sheen. It was knee length, with a high neck, long sleeves, and an appliquéd rectangle of ivory lace on the chest. Feminine, but not sexy. It showed nothing. I commented that I liked it, but I meant in an objective aesthetic sense, not necessarily for myself.

Perhaps I said it out loud to test us. Despite my new look, I could somehow picture myself in this dress, this strange costume. If Eric also liked it, I would buy it and wear it that week in New York and everything would be fine between us.

He did like it. I too needed warm clothes while visiting, we reasoned, as we brought it to the register. At the last moment, he added an over-priced black sweatshirt that I'd also been eyeing. He looked great in it—it reminded me of a black-and-white photo of him from before we'd met. He was in a baggier sweatshirt with a skateboard logo on the front, his hair cropped close to his head, smiling bigger than I'd seen him smile in any other photo, his blond hair all shine. It had never been that short since we'd been together and I always imagined how it might feel to touch it when I looked at that photo. It seemed like it would be soft. Like a pet.

Eric and I walked hand in hand down the street, and a woman with wavy black hair stopped him to say hi. "This is my partner," he said, gesturing to me.

"She's in the program," he told me a few blocks later, as we stopped to look in the window of a Victorian-style ice cream parlor.

"I noticed you called me your partner," I said.

"Yeah, I'm trying it out."

*Partner* was the accepted term at the Whitney for the many participants who were queer and even for some of the straight ones who were married. I think Eric was embarrassed to call me his wife around his new peers.

I liked that he was trying out *partner*. For one thing, *partner* felt more gay, and also, the terms *husband* and *wife* had felt too old for me when I'd married him at twenty-three. I'd liked *girlfriend* and *boyfriend* better.

People use the word *fiancé* to describe the person they are going to marry, but I'd rejected the term. I'd felt that women used *fiancé* as a way to brag about having found a mate. These were the same women who ran around thrusting their engagement rings out at people. Begging to be seen. Begging to be recognized as having won a prize or passed a test. Now I realize they were just happy.

I'd paused my communication with Elena while I was in New York in an effort to direct all my attention toward Eric. I'd told her in advance

I'd be doing this, and she said it made sense. But even when I wasn't talking to her, she was there in song lyrics at coffee shops, in lesbian haircuts on sidewalks.

At the end of my trip, at the gate at JFK, I got a long email from her with the subject line *Strict Diet*.

She had written to me all five days I'd been gone but had disciplined herself not to send the messages. Instead, she saved them into one long email and sent it fifteen minutes before I took off. Her timing and control amazed and frightened me.

*I miss you badly. Need to find a way of not thinking of you every minute. You are having your time with your husband and there is no space for me, which is totally understandable . . . but that thought is poisoning my head. Knowing I'll never be your priority kills me today.*

I didn't have to smoke these words. They found their way inside immediately and burned in my chest, drew heat to my face, echoed in my ears. *There is no space for me. There is no space for me.*

She was right, but I couldn't admit it to her yet. I thought confirmation would only hurt her more. I couldn't quite admit it to myself, either, because I wished it could be otherwise. That there could be infinite space. That no one would be edged out. Before the flight attendant made me turn off my phone, I typed her a message.

*There is space for you. In the gaps of my broken Spanish. In the back pockets of your jeans I'm wearing. There is space in the empty seat across the aisle on this flight; the middle one, between the man in A and the woman in C, who can't seem to open her tiny bottle of wine. If I were filling that space, I'd use my strong hands to help her on her way to getting drunk.*

*I'm good at opening things.*

Zeus said that if the humans didn't behave after he divided them, he'd have to divide them again, leaving them each with only one leg to hop around on. This division wouldn't have fazed me back in my ballerina days. I was pretty good on one leg. When I did pirouettes in class, sometimes I could complete seven rotations atop my tiny satin pointe shoe tip.

I didn't need Zeus to cut me in half, though; I was doing his job for him. I had one foot in Eric and the other in Elena, doing the splits.

In ballet, the more flexible you are, the better, but sometimes being too flexible signals a connective-tissue condition that makes you more prone to injury.

*That wasn't me*, people say. *That must have been my evil twin.* I want to believe it was my evil twin who brought Elena to our house while Eric was away. The evil twin who told her she would never come before him.

I did those things. Does that make me the evil twin?

I want to believe in evil twins because that means there are good twins too. I might glimpse mine in a crowd and chase after her, or I might literally run into her on a city street, our identical exteriors colliding and cracking open, the badness and goodness inside each of us mixing.

At the office, Ethan was frazzled after my weeklong absence. Normally I did most of the interfacing with my boss. Contrary to what I'd heard about women in business, my boss was more willing to hear my opinions than those of men. I think he saw other men as competition, even if they were his underlings. His inability to see me as a threat made him more open to my opinions. Or maybe he just respected me more than he respected Ethan. Whatever the case, when I wasn't there, things were more difficult.

Ethan had a lot to juggle. He was an adult with a job, a marriage, a mortgage, children. David's lack of respect was getting to him. He was outgrowing the supportive but infantilizing nature of this full-time employment but he wasn't ready to give up the job.

He thought a Volkswagen camper van might be the solution. We were in advertising, after all. Even though we were the architects of these empty promises, we weren't above them. Our vocation had soaked into our subconscious, leading us to believe that something we purchased could cure us.

He could use the van to escape, to get back to nature, to take his kids camping at a moment's notice, the way his parents had done when he was growing up. He was looking for a 1996 model, the last year VW made them.

When he found the one he wanted on Craigslist, we snuck out of the office together to see it, on the pretext of "concepting off-site."

The van was gray, and German in its boxiness and ingenious use of space. There was a foldout table and a hot plate hidden under the seat that plugged into the cigarette lighter. The camper top popped up to create a sleeping loft. My childhood camping dream: a whimsical tent inside a vehicle, safe from bugs and snakes.

The man selling it thought we were a couple, because what else are a man and a woman, roughly thirty years old, looking to buy a van and talking about how the kids will like it? It felt strange to have someone assume this about us, oddly like a betrayal to Eric. But it felt innocent at the same time, to let the unspoken assumption go unresolved.

The van drove well. Ethan liked it, and I did too. He told the man he'd be back with a cashier's check to buy it, and I felt sad that it wouldn't be mine too.

"We can concept in it!" he said. "We can start a mobile ad agency and travel around the country in the van, working jobs here and there."

"Let's do it," I said.

In the space between his suggestion and my reply hung the sorrow of knowing that the reality was so much more complicated than the fantasy. We laughed. What else could we do?

*I've thought several times since you left that you have a kind of sadness about Elena*, Eric wrote. I told him he was right, that it upset me to know I was responsible for other people's suffering, or their happiness, for that matter. I was talking about both of them.

*That's what it is to connect with someone*, he said. *At least that's part of it. If I gave you no happiness, what would be the point of our relationship?* It was obvious but true. And despite some difficult moments during our visit, I got a lot of happiness from him. In our silly talk, our sex. The art he exposed me to. The way I could completely relax while he led me around New York, a city he now knew better than I did.

*I was tired of depending solely on you for my happiness*, I said. *It felt too dangerous. I thought if I spread myself around I could be more independent. But that has its inherent problems too. More people to disappoint.*

At the Whitney they'd been reading Marx, and Eric talked about how the capitalist drive for individuality and self-improvement are meant to make people feel alienated and unhappy so they'll consume more.

*What's the answer, then?* I said, slightly annoyed that he was filtering our experience through this lens and intimidated because I knew nothing about Marx.

*I don't know*, he said, *but I do know that withdrawing from your feelings and trying not to be affected by others won't make you . . .*

Me: *Self-sustaining?*
Eric: *Whole.*

*Well, if that's the case, we should all be fine with the open relationship*, I wrote, knowing it was a ridiculous thing to say. We both laughed our textual hahas. *If only it were that easy*, I said.

*I know*, he said. *It confuses me to no end. But I like puzzles.*

He hadn't lost his sense of humor even through all of this. It made me miss him.

We were shooting a commercial at a beach in Malibu, just a few miles up the road from our office. This was the beach where they shot *Planet of the Apes*, we were told, and it was often used as a stand-in for the French Riviera. We sat in the new van, our water bottles making long black shadows on the foldout table. The sun was setting over the ocean, the offshore winds grooming the gentle waves into curling-iron barrels. Out the back window of the van there was a different scene—a host of production vehicles, tall and white, carrying metal C-Stands, costumes, lights, and miles of heavy electrical cables, coiled like snakes, or covered by portable speed bumps so no one would trip while walking through the set.

The fantasy of concepting in the van had become a reality, if only occasionally, when we were on location and needed a quiet place to work. On normal days we still went to Swingers, and over plates of scrambled eggs or tofu chilaquiles wrote commercials for hamburgers and cars. Violent video games and flat-pack furniture. It was both easier and harder to concept in the van. It was quieter than the diner, but the beauty of the beach was distracting.

The perpetual motion of work was like being in the ocean. There were waves of TV briefs and radio assignments and billboards and endless social media updates that needed to be written, presentations that needed to be made to bosses and clients, revisions, sometimes complete do-overs, and, finally, approvals. Then there were commercial shoots that needed to be prepped, shot, edited, color-corrected, mixed, and shipped to TV stations. You'd paddle toward these waves, knowing if you didn't come at them with all your speed and strength, you'd inevitably run into the wave head-on, just as it was breaking, and be pushed down to the bottom of the seabed. And then you'd swim to the surface, grateful for that trusty, buoyant surfboard: your partner, leashed to your ankle. But as soon as you pushed the wet, matted hair out of your eyes, you'd see another wave coming toward you. And you'd be tired and you wouldn't want to keep going, but you'd have to, because you didn't want this to be the end. You didn't want this to be it. You had loved ones at home who needed you, who depended on you. And you weren't ready to die anyway, not like this, in the ocean, at work.

"Are you going to the desert soon?" I asked.

"Yeah, but I wanna take the boys to Death Valley. I'm sick of Joshua Tree."

"When?"

"I don't know. I can't leave with all this shit going on right now, but I'm dying to have a break."

It had only been a month since my trip to New York, but I needed one too.

"What if we just left?" I said. "What if we just drove off together right now and went on an adventure and didn't tell anyone where we were going?"

Ethan didn't reply. He was looking out the window at the place where the director and the camera were.

"I mean, Eric wouldn't know I was gone anyway, as long as I called him every now and then."

"Should we be paying attention?" he said.

"We're fine. They're not gonna start shooting until the sun gets lower."

His phone rang and it was his wife. He slid open the side door of the van and jumped out. I watched him walk slowly around the parking lot while he talked, unreasonably irritated that he took her mundane calls more seriously than our fantasies.

I imagined driving north on the Pacific Coast Highway toward Big Sur, or east toward Death Valley, but it was no fun imagining it alone. I wanted Ethan to build on the story with me, like an exquisite corpse. I wanted to pass it back and forth and see it get wilder with each iteration. I felt safe within the boundaries of this narrative, but maybe it didn't feel that way for him.

I had stopped wearing mascara when I met Elena. I was tired of the way it made me look like a sad clown when I washed my face, and I'd admired the way she didn't try to make herself more beautiful with makeup.

Still, I was obsessed with Ethan's lashes. They were thick and dark—the kind of eyelashes women say are wasted on men. Sometimes I stood over his shoulder when he wanted my opinion on a design or layout, and looked down onto his lashes, fanned out at the edge of his lids like tiny black combs. I imagined kneeling down and turning his chair toward me, our faces close, so I could lay my lashes on top of his, moving ever so slightly to the right or left, until they clasped together like hands in prayer, the tiny hairs interlocking in a black-brown boy-girl eye zipper. We'd blink a kind of handshake, like the butterfly kisses children give, but deeper.

Elena had stopped sending daily pictures of herself and chatting with me online. She had made herself invisible. I missed the days when I could access her just by clicking her name. Often I didn't even get the chance to do so. I'd open my computer and she'd pop up in a window almost immediately. *Hola profesora*, I'd say. *Hola linda*, she'd reply.

It drove me mad, not knowing if she was there and hiding, or gone completely. I tried to follow her lead and respect her feelings, to give her space. I didn't try to communicate; I waited. She only texted when the moon was full, and again when she was getting her period.

*La sangre viene*, was all she wrote, and I responded in kind. At first our *sangre* came at the same time, as though we were injured, waves of blood cresting on our shores. It was comforting to think of her, across an entire continent and ocean, with the same bloated belly, the night sweats, the same red in the toilet. To feel that we were under the sway of the same celestial body. By the next month, the orbits of our menstrual cycles were no longer in sync.

We stopped talking about our periods and talked only about the moon, predictable and distant.

A book arrived in the mail. A hardbound copy of *Bartleby & Co.* by Enrique Vila-Matas, with a note from Elena. *Go to page 234*, it said, and I did.

> [Pineda] produced cigarette-paper from his pocket and without pausing wrote a complete poem . . . which shortly afterwards he made into a cigarette and calmly smoked.
>
> When he had finished smoking it, he looked at me, smiled and said:
>
> "What matters is that you write it."

I hadn't even started my rolling-papers novella. I'd never had idle hands. I'd been too busy juggling her and Eric. When she'd been staying with me, I'd wanted to film her smoking, so the day before she left, I had scribbled a possible first line on a single rolling paper and asked her to smoke it.

*They call me Llorarita—"the little crier" in Spanish.*

She'd been seated at the same table where I'd photographed her the summer before, looking out the window at magic hour. I waited all day for that particular light, warm and cool at the same time. The smoke exhaled from her mouth was white against the shadows on the wall behind her. In my haste I forgot to offer her the ashtray and her ashes fell directly on the table.

The character of Llorarita had come to me while Elena was visiting. We had gone to see friends of hers from film school who'd just had a baby and were living in a trailer on their family's ranch in Ventura County. We cooked outdoors and listened to coyotes, and the mother told me the story of the baby's birth. I cried silent tears and hoped they might go unnoticed in the dark. I didn't think I was the kind of person moved by these sorts of things. The mother saw them first. *Llorarita*, she said, warm and soft, caressing me with this moniker. Elena smiled and nodded and stroked one of my cheeks with the back of her hand.

In the novella, I imagined that Llorarita could quench the thirst of an entire city during a drought with only her tears, but she was tired of how much people needed her to cry. She couldn't cry at the usual things, either—only at books and movies, at architecture. She'd fallen in love with a woman who didn't try to catch the droplets that fell from her lashes even though she was parched. But in the end it became clear that this new lover needed her tears too.

Elena sent me another cryptic message, this time via email. She said she wished that she, Eric, and I could each be like a single die, rolling a one. Each of us having equal status in our relationship. Despite Eric's warning about individuality being a capitalist trap, I liked the thought. I wanted to be a single die.

I went to a hobby store and purchased three loose dice in primary colors. *Dice* is a conjugation of the verb *decir*, which means *to say* in Spanish, and although I had known that before I met Elena, I'd used it more with her than I had anywhere else. *Como se dice?* How do you say? I was hoping the dice would tell me something.

That night, I set up a video camera and filmed the table as I threw them all at once to see if I could roll three ones. I shook the dice in my hand and tossed them out.

1, 3, 5
2, 5, 6
3, 1, 1
6, 3, 4
2, 2, 2
4, 6, 1

I rattled them in my loose fist, and threw them again and again and again. My body cramped, but I kept going until it happened. After fourteen minutes, I rolled three ones.

I sent the entire excruciating video to both Elena and Eric, even though I wasn't sure what it meant. It was the first time I'd emailed them both at the same time.

*How could she have you equally without you leaving me?* Eric asked. I had already tried to figure out this math, but could not.

In addition to the dice analogy, Elena had mentioned wanting to come to LA for a longer period of time; she'd rent her own apartment instead of staying with me. *How do you feel about that?* he asked. My first impulse was to think about how he'd feel, because the answer was more obvious. Instead, I pushed past my telepathy with him and thought about what I really felt.

*I'm realizing it's more than I want*, I said, and was surprised by the relief of admitting this. I had assumed that giving up on my radical, sci-fi ideas about relationships would make me feel like a failure. Instead, I felt like a human rather than an automaton.

*Good*, he said, *because it makes my stomach flip.*

I didn't want less of a relationship with Eric than I already had. I didn't want to risk throwing away the ten years of work we'd done together—work I felt most people wouldn't have bothered to do with me. A relationship of three equals was out of the question for him, and despite the theatrical satisfaction of my dice throwing, I didn't know how to make it work either. Still, I hoped there was some other arrangement, some other way, because I didn't want to let Elena go. I felt twinned with her and wasn't ready to divide, to separate, but the most I could offer her were quick trips, glimpses of each other, and if that wasn't enough, I didn't know what else I could do. *Sorry*, I said to Eric, *I'm talking this out like I'm saying it to her.* I knew he was annoyed that I wouldn't swear her off completely, but he didn't say so.

*It's good to rehearse*, he wrote.

In ballet I had always liked the performance, but never the class. The show, but not the work. But here I was, going over it again and again, sweating it out, trying to get better. Maybe I was evolving.

That evening, Elena's image materialized on my screen. I didn't recognize the wall behind her. It was bare, and the round table where she sat was also foreign. "Where are you?" I said.

"Madrid," she said, swallowing the final *d* completely. Her tone was that of a cop or detective on a television show. *He's dead*, the actor says. Casual, but hoping to shock at the same time.

"*¿Por qué?*"

"Working on my film *en casa de mi hermano*. Needed to get out of London."

It was the film she'd started working on when she stayed with me. It was about immigration, but also about another of her impossible loves, the one before me, who'd been sent back to South America after her student visa had expired. It would be animated, like her first.

She lit a cigarette, squinting as she took a drag on it, and exhaled smoke, glaring at me. This gaze made me fidgety. I was conscious of my own image on the screen, the small picture-in-picture in the larger video chat window. I put my eyes back on hers, but trying to meet her gaze with the webcam was always difficult.

"What?" I said to her stare.

She shook her head slowly. Then she stopped. Kept smoking, kept staring.

I squinted back, mocking her serious face. I thought it would lighten the mood, but it did not. She took another drag of her cigarette.

"Come to Spain," she said. "I'll work, and you can write. I'll take care of you."

"You know I can't do that."

"Why not?"

"I can't leave my job."

"You wouldn't be leaving forever. You'd just be coming here for a little while. You're too good to waste your time forever in advertising."

These were compliments, but they didn't feel particularly kind.

"I can't do that," I said, glancing at my own face in the bottom right corner. Watching myself say these things made them seem more definitive. "That would be the end of me and Eric."

"Not necessarily."

"It would. I can't do it."

"It's not that you can't do it. It's that you won't do it."

"Okay, fine," I said. "I won't do it."

We hung up shortly after that. There was nothing left to say, really. I closed my laptop, wandered around the living room, gazed out the windows. They were dirty and rain-stained even though it hadn't rained in months, not since Elena had been in LA the first time, almost a year before, when there had been many days of thick, desperate rain. I wandered over to the front door, checking to make sure it was locked, as I often did when I was feeling anxious. It was, both the knob and the deadbolt. I leaned my upper back against the cool sturdiness of it. I slid down and got to my knees, slowly lowering my entire body to the floor. I turned my head so that one side of my face pressed into the carpet. If someone had seen me lying there, they might have thought I'd come home from a long day at work, put down my imaginary briefcase like a proper 1950s man, and said, "Honey, I'm home!" Then fallen, face-first, onto the floor, dead.

I was not dead. But I did stay there a long time, breathing in the dirt and dust I'd tracked in on my shoes.

Sometimes I did wonder: If suddenly I couldn't support Eric, would I lose him altogether? Would he put up with my bullshit if I was also a struggling writer or artist, with no emotional or financial security to offer?

Occasionally, it did feel difficult to support him—when I felt hobbled by work, when it ate up all my time and energy. I felt like I was taking care of everything. Who was taking care of me?

I didn't want to be taken care of by Elena. What I wanted was to be her. To be self-sufficient. She worked freelance jobs, and in between took long periods of time off to work on her films. It didn't seem like tearing herself in two, the way I envisioned it would for me, to work in advertising and write books or make movies on the side.

The idea of allowing myself to be taken care of was beyond me. *Cuídate. Take care of yourself.* That was what Elena had said to me at the end of our last call.

I tried to contact Eric the next morning but he wasn't online until much later than usual. When he appeared, I was at work, so I instant-messaged to ask how he was doing. He said he was hungover.

> Me: *What'd you get into last night?*
> Eric: *Oh brother . . . I took someone home.*

He only told me her first name. I didn't ask for her last. I didn't want to be able to look her up, worried about what I'd find. Instead I relied on what he would tell me about her.

He said she was petite and that she lived in London. He said she had an accent and pale skin with freckles, dark brown hair, and breasts larger than mine.

Much later when I mentioned these features to him, he seemed confused. He claimed her breasts weren't particularly large, nor was her hair particularly dark.

Did I make this up? Was I thinking of Elena's breasts? Of their weight and softness? Confusing her translucent skin for the skin of this other woman?

There are three things I know for sure: (1) She was a performance artist visiting New York for a weeklong festival. (2) The night they met, they got kicked out of a gay bar for making out. (3) They had sex.

*I hope that's okay*, he iChatted.

*It's fine,* I typed back. *As I've always said, it's up to you.* I asked if he felt okay about it and he said that he did, especially now that he knew I wasn't upset.

*I'm really grateful for your understanding,* he said. *You are too amazing.*

His compliments helped temper the feelings that were simmering deep inside. Something geologic was happening, but for now I could still put a stopper on it.

Two strange coincidences. First: Like me, the performance artist had been a ballet dancer in her youth. Were we interchangeable? Different versions of the same person? Second: She currently lived in the same neighborhood as Elena. Maybe *they* were interchangeable, playing the same role in our relationship. I wondered how Eric and my trip to London might have been different for him, had he already known her. How it would have been different for me.

*We could start a commune there*, he joked. *Or at least take a visit together.*

I wasn't interested in returning to London now that my relationship with Elena was over. I wanted to go to a country where they spoke Spanish, to continue to improve my skills. Elena and I had talked of visiting her friends in Buenos Aires, but I knew now that would never happen.

*She wants me to come to Istanbul with her*, Eric said. *She's going to move there in a few months. It's the new Berlin or something.*

I punctuated my responses with exclamations. *Whoa! Oh wow! Haha!* I wanted to be supportive in the way he had been with me. I wanted to look excited. And I was, at an atomic level. It felt like everything inside me was dividing and dividing. Like it was all going to come apart.

The following evening, he told me they'd spent the day together, shopping for books and going to a lecture. *A small part of me is worried about getting too attached to her*, he wrote. *We fit each other so well, and that's rare, as you know.*

I did know. I tried to stay calm, acting like a coach or a big sister instead of a jealous lover, a role he'd never played with me. I tried to give him the tools I'd used with Elena. I told him how I frequently reminded myself that what I was feeling was new relationship energy, and that I was conscious of the need to balance it with the old relationship energy I had with him. The ORE, like the raw material you pull out of the ground. Sometimes you have to dig deep for the things you depend on: comfort and security.

*I don't want to give that up for NRE alone*, I said. *Me neither*, he echoed.

*As long as you still love me, I'm happy*, I said. *At this point.*

*Of course*, he said. *I feel guilty having so much pleasure, though. How can one person be so fortunate?*

I too had felt this way, in disbelief about the abundance of love; guilty that I didn't deserve it. *But I got over it*, I told him. *Good to hear*, he said, and laughed.

Looking back, I might have described the feeling differently, less positively. Rather than abundance, I had felt surrounded by love.

The more worried Eric seemed, the more worried I became. It manifested as a pain in my ribs, on the lower right side, the same little knives stabbing from within I'd felt when I had shingles. But no lesions came. I thought about the man who'd had a pain in the same place. The one who had his twin removed. My worry grew teeth and hair. It bit and tangled me.

I needed reassurance that loving this woman didn't make him love me less, just as loving Elena hadn't diminished my love for him.

*I have an incredible time with her*, he wrote, *but it does change how I feel about you.*

Whoa! Wow! Ah! Ha!

*I mean, it doesn't. Sorry, massive typo.*

I couldn't believe he'd left off the *n't* by accident. But I know fingers can move quickly, quicker than mouths can form words. I imagined her mouth on him. His hands on her. And of course, I wanted to know if it had been good. *It was*, he said. And I didn't just want to know if it was good. I wanted details, I wanted moments, I wanted snapshots and sound bites that I could scroll through in my head, alone in my apartment. They helped soothe the pain in my ribs, which only went away when I lay on my stomach and masturbated myself to sleep.

I always thought of her. An individual *o* to his individual *e*. Not fused like we had been for so long. Our ligature was fracturing.

I cursed myself for being a hypocrite. I cursed myself for being weak and afraid. At the same time, I was grateful for the opportunity to learn my limits, because it was there in the outer reaches that I finally encountered my feelings. I wasn't just afraid of being alone. I was afraid of losing Eric, and I told him so.

But I wouldn't tell him to stop seeing the performance artist. I felt I owed it to him to have this experience with her, even if, or perhaps *because* I found it so difficult. She was going back to London soon, so I resigned myself to struggling through her last few days in New York.

I was also struggling with my desire to contact Elena. I wanted to tell her that I finally understood how she and Eric had felt, but I didn't know what good it would do either of us. *I don't need to bring her into this crisis*, I told Eric.

> Eric: *Is it a crisis?*
> Me: *I knew you were going to ask that. My body is telling me it is.*
> Eric: *Then it is.*

I asked what his body was telling him about the performance artist. *I think I need to be more honest with her. More open.* He had told her he was married and that our relationship was open, but I sensed that he hadn't talked much about it, or me. I reminded him that I'd never hidden my commitment to him from Elena.

*I know*, he said. *None of this is easy. Well, some of it is. My love for you.*

Those words gave me some relief. We decided we would regroup after she went home. By another strange coincidence, I was due to arrive in New York the day after she left. I'd had the ticket for ages. There would be no way for us to cross paths, which was fine with me. I wanted her to remain a ghost. She was more manageable that way.

During the final days of her visit, Eric didn't answer his phone very often. I lived those days in a kind of purgatory, hovering between fear and fantasy. Now that I'd severed my ties with Elena I had little to ground me, and I could only masturbate so much.

Here is something that might have soothed me: Barthes says the lover's anxiety is the "fear of a mourning which has already occurred, at the very origin of love ..."

He borrows this idea from Winnicott, who says fear of a breakdown is fear of a breakdown that has already occurred. This breakdown is always some kind of rupture with the mother, a *primitive agony*, and because it happens at such an early age, it is impossible for the baby to process. Losing a twin must produce the same cycle of agony.

Or perhaps it's relief. "Don't be anxious anymore," Barthes counsels; "you've already lost him/her."

The night of my arrival, Eric and I had sex in his tiny Brooklyn bedroom, and I asked him to tell me everything he'd done with the performance artist. "Are you sure you want to know?" he said. I was sure. "Well, for one, she asked me to fuck her against a hard surface."

His bedroom door was open a crack, and I could see a table in the living room with a bright yellow Formica top. I held it in my gaze and imagined her/me being flattened against the cold, hard plastic. Asking for it.

Eric had new undershirts. He'd always worn a crew neck, which showed under his buttoned shirts, and now he had three or four V-necks, which I noticed each time he got undressed.

"When did you get those?" I asked.

They'd bought them together while she was visiting. She said his chest hair was sexy.

After being with Elena, I'd stopped shaving my pubic hair into the landing strip I'd started in college. That awful little Hitler mustache surrounded by sandpapery stubble. Elena's was natural, so I let mine grow. There was comfort in matching, and I realized the pleasure that could be had from hair matted down by wetness touching other hair matted down by wetness.

She also made me less ashamed of my mustache by showing me hers. She sent me photos of herself between waxings or bleachings, looking as sexy as ever. *Con bigote*, the subject line read. Her mother didn't like it when she let her mustache go, she said. Their relationship seemed so easy to me, and I was reassured by the fact there were things her mother didn't like. I still wanted to camouflage my mustache, but finding it sexy on other women was a step toward finding myself sexy.

"How come you never listened to me when I told you your chest hair was sexy?" I asked Eric as we lay in bed.

"Did you ever?"

"I always said it looked fine."

Maybe fine wasn't enough. Maybe I didn't have the chance to love his chest hair until he showed it. And maybe I couldn't have loved it until I loved my own hair.

"Well, anyway, I always told you to get V-neck undershirts, so I'm happy someone talked you into it. Even if it wasn't me."

I slipped my hand under the neckline of the undershirt and felt the warmth of his body. It was no longer my body. I wanted it.

"I'm a bit worried we're trying to make our relationship more sexy at other people's expense," he said.

I'd been so focused on what I could learn and become around Elena, I hadn't thought about it this way.

I was discouraged by my callousness, but I was also encouraged by the fact that we wanted our relationship to be sexy. That we weren't content with its filial charms alone. His fling had reinvigorated my passion for him, but I worried that if it stopped, so too would this heat.

Ethan was coming apart. He bit his fingernails down further. He got into arguments with people at work. One night he left in a huff and called minutes later. "Come with me," he said. "We'll start our own agency, be our own bosses." He had a potential client he couldn't tell me about yet. I called Eric and talked to him in a low voice from behind the glass door of my office.

"But I thought you wanted to be less involved in advertising, not more," he said.

He was right. I fantasized about a day where I wouldn't have to write commercials and could instead write books. Why was I even considering leaving the agency to join Ethan? I looked down at my arms and hands, and imagined all the tattoos I hadn't gotten because Eric didn't want them. Just as I had mistaken Eric's body for mine, for a moment I had confused Ethan's dreams for my own.

Weeks passed and Eric still hadn't mentioned anything about the performance artist, so I cautiously asked whether they had been emailing. He said she hadn't contacted him since she got back to London.

I was envious of her restraint, her lack of neediness. I would have emailed immediately. This was what I'd done with Eric, with Elena. I always dove in headfirst without checking the depth, the safety of the situation.

There was an edge to his voice, an anger that told me he was hurt by her silence, so I suggested he reach out to her, to gain closure, if nothing else. He did, and she responded, saying that this kind of relationship wouldn't work for her. She needed to cut it off, to cauterize the passion between them, before it became a gaping wound. These are my words, not hers.

A mixture of relief and sadness coursed through me. We had dodged this bullet as we'd dodged Elena's.

But what if they weren't bullets? What if they were tiny invisible arrows lodged somewhere in our bodies?

We floated through the house of *us*, shutting doors but not locking them. For the moment things were quiet—there were no other lovers in the picture—and I wondered if this was an opportunity, or even a sign, that we should close the open relationship for now.

I'd always assumed that if I suggested it, Eric would immediately oblige. He didn't. Instead he seemed to want to prove to me that the open relationship didn't work in an absolute way, so I wouldn't try to reopen it when my fear subsided or I met someone else.

*Openness is not self-regulating*, Eric wrote in an email. *Adam Smith was dead wrong to think the invisible hand of the market would save us. A great deal of work must be put into keeping it on track, continually adjusting the terms of the openness. Maybe the Whitney has distorted my mind, but this makes sense to me.*

I was tired of these Marx references. They felt cold and impersonal, but I appreciated the elaborate lengths he was going to. We had iChat summits, three- and four-hour-long conversations about possible controls we could put on future secondary relationships, but we could not agree on what those might be, and negotiations broke down.

Eric invoked another discipline: architecture. *The world just isn't built for this kind of relationship*, he said. *It's not set up for it on any level. Even down to architecture.*

I was frustrated by this argument too. I imagined the suburban tract homes of postwar America—houses built for a mother, a father, and two point five children. *We never wanted to live in one of those houses*, I said. We had always wanted an Eames, a Corbusier, a Mies van der Rohe. We scoffed at people who said, "Those are beautiful, but how can you live in them?" *I know*, he said. *But do you see what I'm saying?*

I couldn't fight anymore. I felt exhausted. *I give up*, I said. *Let's give this monogamy thing a try.* It sounded like a relief. But I didn't want to be naive to think it would solve all our problems.

*Friends in monogamous relationships are always complaining to me too, you know*, I wrote. *Their relationships aren't necessarily easier than ours. But I guess as long as we're happy most of the time, "working it out" is the best we can ever do.*

*That's very Chantal Mouffe of you ;)* Eric wrote. *She has a theory called Agonism that says there's no such thing as true consensus, but that the struggle for it should be seen as positive.*

These were the magic words, the theory that worked for me. I'd always seen struggle as negative, something to be hurried through on the way to agreement, a state I associated with a deep and pleasing harmony. I had forgotten that harmony requires at least two different voices singing two different notes.

*Agonism* made me think of *Agon*, a ballet by George Balanchine. It is the second entry in *101 Stories of the Great Ballets*. *Agon* was a collaboration with Stravinsky, written during the time when he was shifting his musical compositions away from the diatonic scale he'd used previously, and toward a more complex, atonal twelve-tone one.

The diatonic scale has seven steps. Seven steps like our wedding vows. Five whole steps and two half steps for each octave. In a twelve-tone composition, all twelve notes of the chromatic scale are given more or less equal importance, which prevents the music from being in any particular key.

The music in *Agon* is a struggle. The dancers don't dance with it, per se, but around it, underneath it, through it. The music and the choreography also have equal importance and yet, somehow, they do not compete with each other for the audience's attention. There is no backdrop, no sets, no props, just four men and eight women in practice clothes: black tights over white cap-sleeve leotards for the men, and black leotards over pink tights for the women.

First, there is a dance for the four men, then for the eight women, then for all twelve dancers. Within the three main sections are smaller breakdowns, a pas de deux, a solo or two, but there is never a corps de ballet. No group of dancers who merge their bodies into one and become set dressing. The dancers own their bodies; even when they are together, they are individuals.

The taboo of nonmonogamy had infused every sexual experience with a naughtiness that excited me, but I knew now that I couldn't live with it in the uneven times. If Eric had someone else, I would always want someone else too. I'd constantly need to ground myself with the weight of others, unless I could find another way to increase gravity's pull on me.

And though the idea of monogamy was soothing, it wasn't necessarily arousing. In my fantasies, I liked the idea of being tied down, but I couldn't see this bondage as erotic.

How would I hold on to my queerness, now that I'd let Elena go? *I want to express that part of myself but don't know how, in the context of our relationship*, I wrote to Eric. *I don't even know what that means.*

I had no answers, and it nagged at me. I think we both worried it was impossible to do without dating a woman, which I didn't even want to do at that particular moment. I just didn't want that part of myself to be invisible, to disappear.

*I don't know what it means either*, he said. *But it would be good for you to unravel those desires, I think.*

I felt resistant to this unraveling. If I pulled the yarn at the hem of this desire, I feared it would reduce me to a messy tangle. I didn't have faith that I could knit myself back together.

"I've been seeing a psychoanalyst," Eric told me. A man.

"For how long?" I asked.

"A couple of months."

I felt threatened the way I had when he'd told me about sleeping with the performance artist. I knew that he wouldn't be having sex with his therapist, but I worried that the more he got to know himself, the less he would want to be with me. I tried to combat these fears by relying on an old technique. I copied him. But I didn't buy myself more men's clothes, or cut my hair shorter, or find a performance artist to fuck. I went online to search for my own therapist.

In *Intimacies*, Adam Phillips says that "psychoanalysis is about what two people can say to each other if they agree not to have sex."

I sat in my new therapist's office, noting the various volumes of Freud on the bookshelves and the fleece vest she was wearing. It reminded me of a vest my mother had.

One of the first questions my therapist asked me was this: Can you picture you and Eric as close but separate? I could not. I told her I felt like I'd never even heard those two words in the same sentence. They echoed in my head all afternoon. They seemed important.

I enrolled in a fiction class that took place at the teacher's house in Hollywood. It was difficult to get there during rush hour, and to find the time to do the assignments and read my classmates' work. I started staying up until one or two in the morning and getting up at seven, but it was worth it. I loved being around other writers. I loved having deadlines and an audience. And since Eric wasn't living with me, I didn't feel bad about being gone all day and then spending the rest of the night at my desk.

For our homework one week, the teacher had us read a short story she'd pulled from *The New Yorker*. It was a series of statements written from different points of view. First person, second person, and first person plural. These shifts in perspective shaped the narrative arc of a relationship. She told us to mirror this structure and write a story of our own.

Mine was about two characters based loosely on me and Ethan, and when I read it aloud in class, the teacher liked it, and said I should think about submitting it to some publications. I was skeptical. It wasn't original. I couldn't submit a rip-off.

Instead, I showed it to Ethan. He'd put in notice at the agency, and we didn't have much time left together. He'd refused to fantasize about running away in the van that day. He did want to hear what I'd written, though.

We were closed up in our office late in the day, the skylights gone black. I reached for my backpack, glancing over at his sofa to make sure I saw his identical bag lying there, so I knew I was fishing around in my bag, and not his. There was frequent confusion about whose was whose. I'd unzip the small vertical pocket on the front of the bag, the one he called the vagina pocket, looking for my gum or earbuds, and find his wallet or the keys to his house.

I pulled the papers out and made noise with them until he looked up from his screen.

"Ready?" I said.

"Yeah." He faced me and crossed his legs.

I put on my reading voice. Slightly more projection, a little slower than normal. Longer pauses between sentences.

"I started getting avant-garde haircuts. I used the phrase 'totally' more than I was comfortable with. I relied too much on peanut butter for protein. I wasn't concerned about how often I used porn to masturbate."

He laughed. I continued.

"You hadn't always not drank."

I stumbled a bit through that sentence. I couldn't tell if using the double negative on purpose was interesting or just bad.

"You used an X-Acto knife to pick at the eczema on your palm, and started shaving your head after realizing no pill was going to bring your hair back. No one had ever corrected you when you called barbed wire *bob wire*."

I didn't look up, but I could feel he was smiling.

"I was happy I could dress like myself on the first day of work, and that you were dressed like me too. We didn't always agree on what was funny, but we made each other laugh by repeating the Swedish names of the chintzy furniture we were making ads for. We encouraged people to buy violent video games and eat fast food. I tried not to let it bother me. We came in early and stayed late, but we made an arrangement never to call each other on weekends unless it was an emergency. We decided it was probably better if we didn't become friendly with each other's spouses. You had been burned by this when you'd quit your last job."

New paragraph.

"You probably wouldn't have had a baby so early, but your wife had insisted she be a mom by age thirty. My husband and I didn't have sex. You stopped calling stuff 'gay' after I said it bothered me. I always thought it was weird that you did that, especially since you seemed so gay yourself. Other people around the office thought so too, even though you were married. I could tell by the jokes they made, even if they took great pains not to make them in front of me. They knew I wasn't one of them. I was one of us.

"You tried to be a good sport. You participated in the running joke about the belt you once wore that was made out of a pink necktie. You were starting to win bike races then. I was obsessed with the idea of having a threesome. I accidentally replied all on an email. To nonadvertising people, I qualified what I did as 'not real writing.' You would suddenly ask me someone's name whom we'd worked with for months.

"You were totally exhausted. I was totally distracted. I could totally not stop saying totally. I began an open relationship, and you had another son. *It's so hard, but it's so great, you know?* That's what we told people. We took my car everywhere because your wife always had yours. At work, people waited on us hand and foot. *Can I get you a coffee?* they'd say. *What would you like for lunch?* There were elaborate afternoon cheese plates. I felt guilty about it at first. You didn't understand why. You'd never had a problem with entitlement."

He shrugged and smiled coyly.

"I wanted to tell you I liked girls, so instead of telling you, I asked if you'd ever been with a man. I wanted us to be the same. You told me you had been with men, but you'd never really liked the sex, just the cuddling. I dated a few girls, with my husband's permission, but I prided myself on not falling in love with anyone. I was so sure of myself. But then I met a girl who looked like a boy, and I wasn't sure of anything anymore.

"You had always helped your wife with her small-business ideas, even if you thought they had no potential. You designed pink-and-white business cards for the dog-walking service, a logo for the artisanal baby food delivery van. You liked this work. You were good at it. I told my husband if he wanted to go to art school, he shouldn't compromise his dreams for me, so he moved to New York, and we said we'd stay together. I said I would keep working and support him.

"When our boss tried to give us more money, you took it. I took some and asked for more time off. I wanted to travel. I wanted to write. We got our own office. We got a new title, Associate Creative Director, and were embarrassed when our boss told us to lord it over the others. You decorated your side of the office with furniture from the company we used to do ads for and charged it all to the agency. I still refused to buy a sofa for my apartment.

"I developed a bad habit of buying shoes online and returning them immediately. I told my husband if he wanted to date someone else, he should. I don't think he wanted to, but he did it anyway. He met a girl he really liked, and I was surprised at how much that excited me. But the excitement was not just sexual. There were stabbing pains too."

That was the end of a paragraph. I looked up to make sure Ethan was still with me. I didn't know what he'd make of this next part.

"At a certain point, we touched each other. It was while we were shooting a documentary about the do-gooders who'd won the free-car contest. You stood behind me while we watched a woman talk about the dogs and cats she rescued, tears in all our eyes—the director, the cameraman, the sound guy. We were waiting for the moment when we'd surprise her with the SUV that had space for three large animal crates and a plastic interior that could be hosed down. I reached behind me and put my hand on the fly of your jeans, fingers pointing downward, lightly cupped. It was a joke, something silly, like from a movie, and I did it to make you laugh, but you couldn't laugh because we were filming, and you didn't move my hand. So I kept it there."

That was the end of a paragraph, but I kept my eyes on the paper and read on.

"After the shoot, the crew piled into the van, and we took the way backseat. It was dark, and we each let one hand crawl over each other's laps like spiders. The lighter we touched, the less it was really happening.

"The next day at work, we started talking about it midconversation, as though we'd each already carried out the beginning in our heads.

"'As long as it's only in public, but no one can see,' you said, 'I don't think it's so bad.'

"'Yeah,' I said. 'As long as it never goes any further than that, it's fine.'"

I could feel Ethan's eyes on me. "It's funny," he said. "I had a similar fantasy, but mine wasn't that elaborate."

"Well, that's why it's my story," I said. And read on.

"You never wanted to sit at the communal lunch table at work, so I ate in our office with you. I stopped driving my car. We rode bikes together instead. We dressed alike more and more. I had cut my hair short by then. You said you liked it on me. You also liked it when I wore oxford shirts from the school-uniform section of the boys' department. I liked that you liked these things, because my husband did not like them. It made it easier for me to like them when someone else did.

"The girl and my husband both gave me an ultimatum. I chose my husband because my heart told me to. My eyes did their own thing. They cried and cried, and I was relieved and angry and guilty and sad."

New paragraph.

"You were divided at that point, working with me during the day and on a secret project at night. It was going to be your ticket out. You stopped saying hi when I came into the office in the morning. You were just busy, I told myself. I was good at making excuses for you. We both started seeing therapists. I stopped trying to reason with you when you said you hated your mother. I just let you hate her. One night when we were having one of those long talks in our office, you reminded me you'd been touched by a babysitter, as though you'd already told me before. I guess you thought you'd already told me everything. I didn't have time to question you further because you kept talking. You said you realized you were depending on your wife for too much of your happiness. I understood how you felt. 'It's too much to expect one person to be your lover, your business partner, your friend, and your mother,' I told you.

"'I've been thinking about maybe having a glass of wine now and then, at barbecues and stuff,' you said. 'Does that scare you?'

"'Kind of,' I said. But it was more than that."

I was heading toward the finish line. I kept my eyes on the paper.

"How was it that when we drove back from San Diego in the dark that time, and I put your hand between the V-neck of my shirt and the lace of my bra, that I didn't get us into an accident? How did I almost think about saying yes to leaving the agency and starting our own? I guess I couldn't see myself without you.

"The day you told our boss you were quitting, you left a note on my desk that said, *Thank you. It's meant more to me than you'll ever know.* You thought he was gonna kick you out before you got to see me, but he didn't, he still had work for you to do. I was late that day, and when I got in, you were there, and the note was on my desk, so I asked if I could read it in front of you. You weren't really there anymore anyway, you hadn't been in months. In therapy that week, I had talked about you leaving, but there were no tears. Just words. And the words weren't even damp or drippy. They were more like a dog pacing back and forth behind a chain-link fence. My therapist asked what I'd miss most about you, and I said, 'I don't know, his dependability?' She frowned and said, 'Dig deeper.'"

I paused.

"So, what is the thing you'll miss most about me?" Ethan said.

"Well, first you have to actually leave," I said. "But I'm getting to that."

I went back to the page.

"I didn't have to dig that deep. It was like playing in the sand at the beach.

"'He never asked me to be anything,' I said, tears welling up in my eyes as though I'd raked my hand through the sand at the shore and the seawater immediately filled the hole, creating a little salty pond in the shimmering expanse.

"'He never asked me to be anything other than who I was.' The sentence lay there like a faded old beach towel, messy and crumpled. And as I said it, an errant wave of tears came up and soaked it through, and I sat there, wringing it dry until she said our time was up."

"Read it again," Ethan said.

After a few months of my own therapy, I came out to my mother. And she came out to me. Mine was figurative, hers literal. I was tired of pretending everything was going smoothly with Eric, but to tell her what was going on would mean coming out about my sexuality and also my open relationship. I always thought if I'd been gay, I would have come out to my parents right away and that they would have been supportive. Alex had just come out to her parents and I saw how much happier she was. How much lighter. But it was the open relationship that stopped me. There was no precedent for that. There was no Ellen DeGeneres on the cover of *Time* magazine.

I asked my mother to visit me in Los Angeles. She said, "Dad can't come out, you know. He doesn't have enough vacation." I told her I knew that, and that I wanted her to come on her own.

I'd never seen either of them travel alone, except the times my mother had gone back to Chicago to care for her dying parents. All other travel and vacations were a joint affair. My parents were a unit, and for most of the time I'd been with Eric we'd been a unit too. It had been nearly ten years since I'd spent any time alone with my family.

It was February, and once my mother had spent a night in our barely insulated apartment, warmed only by portable space heaters, she understood what I'd been talking about.

"You weren't kidding," she said. "It's freaking cold here."

It took me a day or two to find the courage to steer the conversation to a place where it made sense to bring up my situation with Eric, my breakup with Elena. I told her about Alex, and Jimena, the girls at the residency. Once I started talking I didn't stop.

She sat down on the edge of the air mattress I'd placed in my living room.

"It's okay," my mom said. "You know I love you no matter what." These were the same words my father would say to me days later on the phone.

I laid my head in her lap. I held on to her waist as my tears soaked her pants.

I could sense she was surprised by my tears, by their force and their wetness. "You know, you don't *have* to tell me all this," she said.

"I want you to know me," I sobbed. "I just want you to know me." I kept saying it. I'd landed on the thing that was true, so there was no point in saying anything else.

"I do want to know you," she said. "I do." She stroked my hair as we sang these lyrics back and forth. The steady movement of her hand was the backbeat of the song, which faded with the light in the windows.

"Will you do the caterpillars?" I started to say, remembering how she used to smooth my eyebrows as a kid. Before I could finish, she was already doing them.

I decided to get another tattoo. My first in eleven years. I didn't tell my mother because I knew she'd disapprove, as she'd disapproved of the others. *Your skin is perfect*, she'd always said in protest. Eric discouraged me with the same phrase, but it didn't matter. That word felt meaningless to me.

I got the word ÊTRE on the inside of my upper arm. A solid rectangle, like a censor bar, with the word made out of the negative space, as though the ink had been rubbed away like a lotto scratcher.

It is a particularly sensitive area, the tattoo artist told me. Even tough guys who are covered head to toe wince. She held my skinny little arm between her much larger arm and heavy breast so I wouldn't flinch while she deposited the ink beneath my skin. There was something maternal about this, and incredibly soothing.

*Être*: the infinitive form of *to be* in French. Before it is conjugated, conjugal. Before it is married to *me* or *you*, *he/she/it*, *we*, *you all*, or *them*.

I'd been surprised at how encouraging Eric had been when I told him about coming out to my parents, but I still sensed a dissatisfaction in him, so I decided to dig. *What are you missing?* I asked.

*Embodied experience with you,* he wrote, *though I'm not even missing it so much, now. But I feel you could live apart like this for the next ten years and be fine with it, and I don't know that I would be okay with that.*

*I don't need more right now,* I wrote. I liked being able to come and go as I pleased, having experiences on my own. I liked being able to write late into the night without feeling guilty.

> Eric: *I know . . . It's true. The freedom I have here has really allowed me to focus on my work.*
> Me: *So, what's the problem, then?*
> Eric: *I'm just stressed because the Whitney is ending in a month and I'm trying to figure out what happens next.*
> Me: *I know you want to live together again, but how can we have all these things under one roof?*
> Eric: *We'll figure it out. We'll have to.*
> Me: *I hope so, because if not, it'll make the relationship unbearable.*

*Oh, just having our relationship would be murder?* he said. Even though they were just words on a screen, I could sense his tone immediately. It was almost like the sentence itself was narrowing its eyes.

*Not murder for me,* I tried to explain, *murder for the relationship.* I didn't want it to die, and I knew that putting it ahead of everything else made me want to destroy it.

Now I see the confusion in our language. I think for Eric, *just having our relationship* meant monogamy, having only one love relationship. For me, *just having our relationship* meant that our love relationship would be *the only* thing I had.

I still faulted monogamy for preventing me from feeling whole on my own. I was protective of my newfound agency and worried that I might kill anything that got in its way.

When Eric was done with the Whitney, I came for the final group show. During his year in New York, he had abandoned the code-based interactive installations he'd made in grad school and begun to take photographs. In the show, he showed three. The first was a still life of a military drone built out of balsa wood. He'd downloaded the plans from the internet, cut the pieces out by hand, and glued them together like the model airplanes of his youth. The second photo was of the white noise machine in the waiting room of his therapist's office. The third was a photo he'd taken years before in LA, but never printed. It was a ghostly, Jesus-like face in the carpet of our apartment, an indentation I'd left after doing a headstand. While I admired his prior work, the spinning threads, and how they responded to people in their intelligent, robotic way, I liked this new work better. Though mysterious, it implied a narrative. It was engaging in a more human way.

That night, we walked home across the Williamsburg Bridge. "How are you feeling about things?" he said.

"Good," I said. "Better." I told him about the pain in my ribs that had returned when he'd met the performance artist and how it had gone away once she had too. We stopped and held each other.

"I'm happy," he said. "I want to be with you. But I think I'd like to stay here a little longer."

I was surprised at his change of heart. "Really? But I thought you wanted to move back in together."

"I do, but I can wait a little longer. I'm scared about moving back to LA right now when things are just starting to happen for me."

He said he'd made more friends in the past year in New York than the previous ten in Los Angeles, and felt he was close to getting a gallery to represent him. I didn't want to take those things away from him, and I was interested in what living apart in a monogamous relationship could be like.

"Let's try it," I said.

When I stopped speaking to Elena, I also stopped speaking Spanish. I missed it as I missed her. When I rode my bike to work, I repeated certain phrases to feel like I was still having the mundane conversations we had when she was staying with me. *¿Qué quieres hacer? ¿Quieres comer algo?* But it wasn't a conversation, of course. *Estoy practicando mi español*, I imagined I'd tell her if we spoke again someday. *¿Con quién?* she'd ask me, to which I'd reply *hablando sola*—a phrase she'd taught me that meant *talking to myself.*

Whether I was alone or not, I felt like another person when I spoke Spanish. My voice became lower, probably mimicking Elena's, since the way I learned was by repeating the words and phrases she taught me. *Is that what I sound like?* people often say when they hear a recording of themselves. It feels separate from the self that made the recording. When I spoke Spanish, I had this experience in real time, the experience of being two people simultaneously.

I heard Elena's voice coming out of my mouth, and that was comforting. Sometimes I'd repeat words or phrases I'd heard her say, even if they weren't accurate. I watched videos of her to feel closer to her speaking voice. *Arrorres*, I'd say under my breath, trying to roll my *r*'s.

*I'll go to Mexico*, I thought. *The Her me can exist there.*

I went through customs at Benito Juárez International Airport, and after showing my passport and thanking the customs agent with a *gracias*, I was instructed to hit a button. It turned green, which meant I was free to go through without having my things examined. I realized as I was passing that I'd said *gracias* like Elena had taught me, with a *th* sound for the *c* instead of an *s* sound, the way Mexicans did it. I was going to have to unlearn that lisp, but I didn't want to. Lisping my *z*'s and *c*'s made me feel like she was still there, emerging from inside me.

Maribel from the photo lab waved and opened her arms. After my breakup with Elena, we'd had coffee together a few times. I had a little crush on her, but she had a boyfriend, which I figured was for the best. "*Holaaa*," she said, drawing out the *a*. She was dressed in jeans, with high-top sneakers and a black-and-white bandana tied around her neck. It looked like something an outlaw or gangster might wear. We hopped in a car she'd borrowed from her *tío*, a tiny silver hatchback called a Volkswagen Polo. It had a fake aftermarket Porsche steering wheel. We spent hours in Mexico City gridlock on the way to her *abuela*'s house, but there were no lapses in our conversation. Midway through our trip, I said, "Let's speak Spanish as much as possible."

"*Pues claro*," she said with a smirk.

There were bunk beds in the bedroom where Maribel and I stayed, although they weren't technically bunk beds because there weren't two of them. There was one lofted bed, and beneath it a floral sofa where I slept. The house was in Coyoacán, which was Frida Kahlo's neighborhood, Maribel told me.

"I'll take you to Casa Azul and you can see where she grew up." I understood almost everything she said, but I wasn't quick enough to respond in any complex way. *Vale* had been my usual response with Elena, a phrase used in Spain for *okay* or *all right*. They didn't use it in Mexico, though. Maribel taught me *órale* instead.

The only decoration on the wide expanse of her dingy white bedroom wall was a circular painting of Elvis, about the size of a vinyl record. It had a hole worn in the middle of it, right between his eyebrows. It was a head-and-shoulders portrait, and you could just make out the neckline of a pale blue shirt and the popped collar of an orange wide-lapeled jacket. This was midcareer Elvis, still thin and unbloated, with shaggy hair that flopped over his forehead and feathered out around his jawline.

I thought it was a strange picture to have, but I never asked Maribel about it—whether she had carried it with her from Los Angeles, or if it had come with the bedroom, a relic of its past inhabitant. Elvis, the surviving twin, kept watch over the two of us, sleeping separately, in a bunk bed and sofa.

Maribel couldn't believe I hadn't heard of Chavela Vargas, the famous Mexican singer of ranchera music.

We were lying on the couch in her bedroom after a long night of drinking and then driving through red lights. This had terrified me, but she claimed that after a certain hour of the night, if you were a woman, this was police-sanctioned behavior (the red-light-running, not the drinking) to help prevent carjacking.

"You haven't heard 'La Llorona'?" she said. I hadn't. Maribel said she was a popular character in Latin American mythology, the ghost of a woman who wandered the streets at night, wailing and crying because she regretted killing her children. One version of the story said that she'd drowned the children because the man she was in love with didn't want them, and the other said she'd been in love with a man who lavished his two children with attention, and that La Llorona had drowned them out of jealousy.

I wondered if Elena's friend had been referring to this character when she'd called me Llorarita.

"Let me find the song for you," Maribel said. "It's amazing." She sat up and opened her computer. I settled back onto the couch while I waited for her to find the song. It was dark outside, and the Christmas lights she had hanging around the top bunk of her bed reminded me of college, or camp. Her legs were spread wide, knees bent at right angles as she leaned forward over the coffee table, a tinge of boyishness coloring her posture.

"Ah, found it," she said, and pressed play. The recording was old and crackly and so was Chavela's deep voice. I watched Maribel's face in profile as Chavela sang.

The song begins with her singing from the point of view of La Llorona.

> *Todos me dicen el negro, Llorona / negro, pero cariñoso . . .*
> They call me the black one, Llorona / black but affectionate . . .

Toward the end of the song, the point of view changes, and she seems to sing *to* La Llorona.

> *Tápame con tu rebozo, Llorona / porque me muero del frío.*
> Cover me with your shawl, Llorona / because I'm dying of cold.

It was as though La Llorona sucked the life out of anyone in her presence. I felt the pain of wanting Maribel to be Elena. The unfairness of it.

The song was a waltz, and I pictured myself dancing to it with an invisible partner, one hand clasping his or her hand, the other around his or her back. One, two, three, two, two, three . . . until suddenly, it crescendoed and abruptly ended.

> *Si ya te he dado la vida, Llorona / ¿Qué más quieres? / ¿Quieres más?*
> I already gave you my life, Llorona / What more do you want? / You want more?

Instead of Casa Azul, we went to the houses where Frida Kahlo and Diego Rivera lived toward the ends of their lives. They are two unadorned two-story boxes on the same property called Las Casas Gemelas. The Twin Houses. They're completely separate, but identical in shape and size. The only difference between them is color: one white and the other blue. I assumed correctly that Frida's was the blue house. This hue could have been an homage to La Casa Azul, the house she grew up in, only a few minutes away, and although she never had a blue period like Picasso, I assigned this color to her because she seemed to be sadder than Diego.

We paid our two hundred pesos and were given a brochure about the houses and allowed to wander through them on our own. We began in the white one, Diego's. The bottom floor housed his studio, where a few of his paintings and drawings were arranged with easels and paintbrushes to approximate the way it looked when he was working there. We walked up the narrow staircase, which turned two right angles in only about twenty steps, to the second floor. We passed a modest twin bed that seemed impossibly small for a man of his size, and we went out the door onto a rooftop terrace.

Maribel got a phone call. I didn't try to understand her conversation. Instead, I ventured out onto the bridge and stopped in the middle, between Diego's and Frida's houses. I was only two stories up, but I imagined myself thirty-five thousand feet in the air, unable to see the ground below. I was on a flight between New York and Los Angeles, between Eric's and my apartments. I felt neither blue nor white, sad nor pure. I felt hopeful.

It seemed that all the buildings in Mexico City had these roof-top terraces. Maribel had taken me to a late-afternoon party at the home of an artist she'd worked for, who was called Diego, like Diego Rivera, and we sat around smoking cigarettes and drinking Victoria beer with a group of their friends. Diego's children ran around, tracking soil between the potted cacti and succulents that littered the terrace. When we left that evening, after the sun had gone down, Diego walked us downstairs and out onto the street. He kissed me once on the cheek. "*Mucho gusto*," he said.

"*Mucho gusto*." I parroted this phrase when people said it to me, understanding that it was the proper thing to say after meeting someone in Mexico.

"Your girl is hot," Diego said in Spanish as he kissed Maribel on the cheek, assuming I wouldn't understand.

"Mm-hm," she said to him, with a little shake of the head and a roll of the eyes. One corner of her mouth turned up, but I couldn't decipher this tick. Was it about me? About him? About them? About us? I decided it meant, "She's not my girl, Diego."

"Diego and his wife have an open relationship," Maribel told me later.

"Does she sleep with other people?" I asked, thinking of Frida Kahlo and her affairs with women.

"I'm not sure," Maribel said, "but Diego and I . . . there's a history there."

*Which one was Diego's wife?* I wondered. Who was the mother of those children running around on the roof that afternoon? The wife of the man who had slept with Maribel. I believe she was at the house when we visited that afternoon, but she is not reliably there in my memory of it. I don't remember meeting her, or if I did, she wasn't introduced as his wife. She could have been the woman with long brown hair, parted in the center. She could have been the woman wearing the hippie dress. She could have been the woman Maribel embraced when we came into the house, but Maribel embraced a lot of people. She kissed a lot of people on one cheek, the way Mexicans do, not twice, like the French or Spanish, and she introduced me to all of them. The names washed over me the way they do when you know you won't need to recall them.

I remember a woman on the roof who was beautiful and serene, if a bit aloof. This could have been her. She did not talk to us after the initial greeting. There were a few clusters of people on the roof that afternoon, and she was not in ours. Maribel and I talked with friends of hers I'd already met, girls she grew up with in Mexico City: a fellow photographer, a jewelry designer, a psychology student. I watched the woman who might have been Diego's wife as she sat and smoked with a group of older people—they weren't that much older than we were, but enough to make a difference—and her children came and went to her. She was the anchor to their tiny ships, which drifted away on various missions to collect bottle caps and cigarette butts. When they returned to her, she accepted them with one arm, without even looking down, with no break in the conversation. It was a gesture so automatic it could have seemed cold, but it didn't. I longed to go to her as well, but I did not.

"What does Diego's wife do?" I remember asking Maribel as we smoked on the roof that afternoon. I remember five answers she may have given:

*She's an artist as well.*

*She's a photographer.*

*She's a writer.*

*She takes care of the kids.*

*She does a bunch of things.*

I have no idea which of these it was.

Is it too hard for one relationship to sustain two artists? Was that what made Diego Rivera and Frida Kahlo's relationship so tumultuous? What about the other Diego and his phantom wife? Was their relationship also a competition for personal and artistic recognition?

Three more things about Diego and Frida:

Diego had a twin who died when he was two years old.

Diego and Frida divorced in 1939, but remarried a year later in San Francisco, while he was working for the Golden Gate International Exhibition. They remained together until Frida's death in 1954.

Diego indicated that when he died, he wished for their ashes to be commingled. This wish was not honored. He was buried instead in the Rotunda of Famous Men.

I had to hire a Spanish-speaking writer because most of our clients needed ads in both languages. It was oddly difficult to find this person. Much of advertising relies on humor, but it often doesn't communicate across language and my Spanish wasn't quite good enough to get the nuance of jokes. I found a writer who'd made lots of Spanish ads but had also written, produced, and starred in an English-language web series about trying to meet his celebrity crush, a hot girl I'd seen in a few movies.

When he came for the interview, I felt like I was meeting Ethan again. He was slight of build with dark brown hair and the "gay voice" that had led me to believe Ethan was closeted. And like Ethan, he had a girlfriend who'd be moving to LA with him. I offered him the job, excited at the prospect of using my Spanish on a daily basis with someone other than a lover.

After months of working together, occasional mentions of male celebrities he drooled over, and performative swoons at certain male actors in our callback sessions, he came out to me. Over iChat, of course. *You know I'm bi, right?* he said. *So am I!* I typed back without thinking. *Really?* he said, and followed it with a paragraph's worth of alternating question marks and exclamation points.

I told him I had thought he wasn't straight, but hadn't wanted to breach the boss/employee boundary by asking. *Bilingual and bisexual*, we joked. He was seven or eight years younger than I was, but this revelation melted those years away. He was very comfortable with his sexuality, he said, and planned to come out to the other creatives too. He was frustrated by the invisibility of male bisexuality, upset that gay people saw his relationship with his girlfriend as a way to stay closeted and that straight people assumed his happy, monogamous relationship meant he only liked women. He inspired an immediate urge for imitation. I told him I would come out to the others at work too. The time had never felt right before, but I realized I had to make a time for it to be right.

We talked more over the following weeks, and found that while we both liked men and women, our bisexualities were much different. He liked the ends of the spectrum, masculine men and girly girls, whereas I was more interested in androgyny. I preferred the term *queer*, anyway. Bisexuality felt too narrow, too binary, and too sullied for me. He said it worked for him. I liked the fact that we didn't agree. I felt the warmth of solidarity within the difference of our sameness.

We both posted on National Coming Out Day, knowing our colleagues would see the updates, and I found that claiming my identity with words was as exhilarating as it was with flesh.

We all sat at the conference table late one night, listening to my boss rehearse his part of a pitch presentation. "The job of advertising is to persuade people to prefer one brand over another," he began. I mouthed his words to myself, etched into me as they had become, like a vinyl record. I'd seen this presentation a hundred times, because he told each potential client the same thing: "People can't have a preference if they can't see a difference."

The first time I heard this line, I was struck by its truth. How elegant it made the obvious. And unlike so many things, subsequent repetitions did not diminish it.

In *One and the Same*, the first book I'd read that mentioned Vanishing Twin Syndrome, Abigail Pogrebin writes of a 1954 study by the psychologist Dorothy Burlingham in which she concludes that mothers can't connect to their twins until they get to know them apart from each other. "Several mothers have plainly said that it was impossible to love their twins until they had found a difference in them."

Eric said he'd made a huge discovery in therapy that revolved around two stories I'd heard before. The first was one his mother frequently told, about how hard it was to wean him. The way she told it, it was he who didn't want to be weaned, but I always suspected she didn't want to let him go, either. The second was one he told about locking her out of the car when she tried to drop him off at school so she couldn't leave him.

Eric had spent every waking moment of the first three years of his life with his mother in a remote town on the Great Plains where his father had taken a teaching job. This intense period of mother-son togetherness ended abruptly when they moved back to civilization and she began waiting tables at night.

Three years, blissfully merged in self-imposed isolation. It was the same amount of time Eric and I had spent in a similar state at the beginning of our relationship.

*I never properly separated from her*, he said. *But recently, I had this strange experience of looking at my reflection in the mirror while I was peeing and these words welled up in me: you have no idea how powerful you are.*

    Me: *While you were peeing?*
    Eric: *No, it was after I peed. Haha.*

What he'd experienced was essentially the Mirror Stage, he said, where the child realizes they are independent and not merged. *The Mirror Stage usually happens around two to three years old, and of course I had that*, he said, *but to a very minimal degree. This was the moment it all crystalized, into my own subjectivity, my own desiring body.* I was struck by how lovely and profound these words were, the picture they painted: precious gems glinting in the sun, a naked body emitting light.

The loveliness gave way to bleakness. *I was infantilized*, he continued. *That's why I just waited for you. I thought if I locked myself away, if I was perfect, you would come back to me.*

I saw a parking lot, a station wagon, tears inside a self-created prison.

*I had suppressed all my own desires, which only made it worse*, he said. There had been an architecture professor who was interested in him during the time I'd been seeing Jimena, before his summer in Maine, but he hadn't let himself flirt with her. *I thought it would keep me close to you. Boy was that wrong.*

> Me: *You should have just flirted with her! Opened the steam valve a bit.*
> Eric: *I know.*
> Me: *That's what we should do in the future.*
> Eric: *It's true. There's nothing wrong with flirting.*

I was sorry I'd played his mother in this painful scene in the car. That I'd helped him reenact it. The station wagon became a boat and I heard my own therapist's voice. *It's so young*, she had said of the terror I felt about separating from Eric. She'd compared me to a little tugboat, tethered to the mother ship, so that I could float off on my own but never have to worry about being lost at sea.

She'd used this image to explain *rapprochement*, I told him. It's part of the separation-individuation phase where the child wanders off but keeps looking back to make sure the mother is still there. *I should have completed it between fifteen months and two years, but I've been repeating it with you.*

Despite the perversity of casting each other in these maternal roles, we were proud of each other, for the work we'd done, and for these revelations. We cried at our screens for a while. I felt relief and joy. I'd never seen Eric cry, really cry, and though I wished he would do it with me, in person, narrating it as it was happening was the next best thing. Like sexting, but with tears.

Eric had just finished *Moby-Dick* and sent me his copy. "Tell me when you get to 'The Squeeze of the Hand,'" he said.

It took me some time. It is chapter 94, and in it, Ishmael describes an ecstatic afternoon spent squeezing lumps out of the sperm that had been harvested from the whale's hump.

> It was our business to squeeze the lumps back into fluid. A sweet and unctuous duty! No wonder that in old times sperm was such a favorite cosmetic ... after having my hands in it for only a few minutes, my fingers felt like eels, and began, as it were, to serpentine and spiralize ... Squeeze! Squeeze! Squeeze! All the morning long; I squeezed that sperm till I my self almost melted into it; I squeezed that sperm till a strange sort of insanity came over me; and I found myself unwittingly squeezing my co-labourers' hands in it, mistaking their hands for the gentle globules. Such an abounding, affectionate, friendly, loving feeling did this avocation beget; that at last I was continually squeezing their hands, and looking up into their eyes sentimentally; as much to say,—Oh! My dear fellow beings, why should we longer cherish any social acerbities, or know the slightest ill-humor or envy! Come; let us squeeze hands all round; nay, let us all squeeze ourselves into each other; let us squeeze ourselves universally into the very milk and sperm of kindness.

I found this scene to be incredibly erotic, though no sex is mentioned at all. Eric agreed.

As the passage continues, Ishmael decides to "lower, or at least shift, his conceit of attainable felicity"—to take pleasure in simple things, "the wife, the heart, the bed, the table, the saddle, the fire-side . . ." The slippery grasp of his fellow sailors' hands.

The word *lower* threatened to depress me so I focused on *shift* instead, and I replaced Melville's simple things with my own. The dance, the partner, the pen, the paper, the story.

When I put away *Moby-Dick*, I found Eduardo Galeano's *Mirrors*, a book Elena had given to me before we broke up. I finally decided to read it. As the subtitle (*A Short History of Almost Everyone*) suggests, it is a series of creation stories. One in particular caught my attention: the myth of the Egyptian gods Osiris and Isis. They were twins, it said, who began making love in their mother's womb and married each other as soon as they were born.

The idea of lovemaking in the womb got me hot. A place that was pre-*mœurs*, where no one could tell you who or what or how you were supposed to fuck.

The story of Isis and Osiris felt like Eric's and mine. We'd brought a primordial relationship out into the world, and tried to keep living it as though we were still in the womb. But our relationship wasn't a baby anymore. It had grown—six years, seven years, eight years, nine. Living apart had been like sending it to boarding school, allowing it to mature on its own. I sent the passage to Eric.

In a future edition of *101 Stories of the Great Ballets*, I imagine an entry for *Twincest*. First presented in a Brooklyn bedroom, starring two dancers: me and Eric.

*Twincest is a dramatic ballet about a Parisian twin brother and sister who are in love with each other. As is common in ballet, though the characters are adolescents, they are played by young adults. It is the 1960s, and the twins are on a monthlong family vacation at a farmhouse in the south of France. As the curtain rises, they are in separate twin beds on opposite sides of the room, listening as their parents return home from a night out. We see their parents, jovial and drunk, retire to their room, adjacent to the twins' room, and after a few moments of attempted seduction, they fall fast asleep. The twins listen; the girl cups her hand to the wall, and once she hears them snoring, she gives her brother a signal. He gets out of bed and crosses the room to join her in hers, lying side by side.*

*Since this ballet is about breaking the ultimate rule of sibling-hood, it also breaks the ultimate rule of ballet: silence. The dancers speak to each other.*

"I'm glad we get to share a room," I say.

"Me too," he says, caressing my shoulder.

"I want you to fuck me."

"Are you sure?"

"Yes. I've listened to you fuck your girlfriends through the wall between our bedrooms. It sounds like they love it and I want to try."

He kisses me and slides his body over mine. The whispers vibrate against our lips.

"Are you ready?"

"Yes."

He is inside me, and it feels better than any time he has been inside me in our real lives, because this fucking is new and secret and forbidden. We are performer and audience to each other.

I come immediately and he does too. It is over. But it is not over. Something has been completed.

We decided it was time to occupy the same space again. We thought it might be part of the cure. No more carpet, we said. No more beige. We needed wood floors, and no one below us.

Eric had gotten what he wanted from New York: he'd been offered a solo show at a gallery on the Lower East Side and could make the work for that show in LA, paying less studio rent than he paid in New York. He'd also taken a contract software job in New York, and with this additional income, we had enough for a down payment on a house.

I found a two-bedroom in the hills of Silver Lake. The sellers were architects, a husband and wife, who had rented half of it during its prior life as a duplex. Eventually, they were able to buy it and turn it into a single-family dwelling. They put in floor-to-ceiling windows to maximize the light and view of the hills, and tore down the wall between the two apartments to make it one open space.

It's like the inverse of twins, I thought. Instead of a dividing egg, it was two eggs fused together.

It was just like the houses Eric had studied in architecture school, the kind we'd driven by and dreamed of inhabiting. We agreed to put in an offer on it, even though he had only seen it in images. "I trust you," he said.

At the inspection, I asked the seller if it had been difficult to turn the two apartments into a single home. "It was tricky," he said. "The wall that separated them was load bearing, so we had to find another type of support so the ceiling wouldn't cave in."

"What did you do?"

"We put a steel band all the way around it," he said.

"What kind of a band?" I asked, imagining something horizontal. The rings of Saturn. A band of quartz in a metamorphic rock.

"Here," he said, and got a Moleskine journal out of his jacket pocket to draw me a picture.

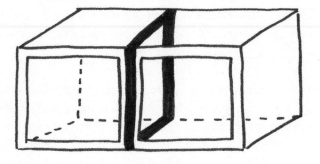

"Ah," I said, sliding an imaginary ring onto my finger. "Like a wedding band."

I bring Eric to our new house for the first time. It is dark inside; the previous owners have taken the lamps. Eric runs his hand along the wall, looking for a switch, and turns on the overhead lights.

It is all the houses we lusted after. The Mieses and Corbusiers; the Philip Johnsons. The kind of house people warned us about—nowhere to hide. We are on display to the houses across the canyon, to people on the street below, to each other. Perhaps we'll thrive under this scrutiny, protected by the watchful eyes of the world. Or maybe the exposure will burn.

The house is an art gallery. Clean lines and white walls. It is the ballet studio of my youth—a rectangle with glass panels on one side. But these are not mirrors. They are windows. We look out, not back.

I drop my bag in the center of the room, and though it's been years, I wind up for a series of fouetté turns.

A fouetté is a one-legged turn, perfect for Zeus's disobedient humans. The ballerina whips one leg in a circular motion from the front to the side and then into passé (toe to knee) while turning and rising on and off pointe on the standing leg. The turns are done in place. She rotates 360 degrees, but she does not roam. Planetarily, it is a series of days, not a year.

In *Swan Lake*, Odile does thirty-two of them. I've read that it's proper to start clapping at twelve. They come at the end of the Black Swan pas de deux when Odile and her partner take turns impressing the audience. Pierina Legnani, an Italian, was the first to perform the thirty-two fouettés in *Swan Lake* in 1895. Italian dancers were more athletic than their French and Russian counterparts and they also knew how to spot when they turned. Spotting means you focus on one fixed point, whip your head around, and return to that point. It keeps you from getting dizzy. In ballet class, you spot your face in the mirror. When you're onstage there is no mirror, just a single red light on the wall at the back of the auditorium.

In the house there is no red light. There is nothing stopping me. I spot Eric's face. I go round and round but I always come back to him. The spotting steadies me.

I can't do thirty-two but I don't care. I stop after six and we laugh. He grabs me and I hold on to him and we sway in the bareness of the room.

Spotting can be a symptom of a vanishing twin. It is only light bleeding. Sometimes they call it *breakthrough*.

Thank you to Yuka Igarashi, Monika Woods, Sarah Manguso, Chris Daley, Darri Farr, Rick Sittig, and everyone on the Counterpoint/ Catapult/Soft Skull team who helped bring this book into the world. To Karolina Waclawiak for publishing my essay on *BuzzFeed*. To my parents for their love and support in all my artistic pursuits. To everyone who provided inspiration and encouragement along the way, especially PV and CW, but also DV, MA, KK, AT, NC, EGS, and ALW. Thank you to John Houck for all of this and more; for your passion and devotion to your work—it makes me take my own more seriously—and for your equal if not greater passion and devotion to me and Freja. We thrive because of your care. Thank you for the ink beneath your skin. A knot that isn't pulled tight, a deliberate mark, a thread, a yarn. Our story on the tenderest part of your arm. I'll trace it over and over.